WILDLIFE
IN COLOR

BY ROGER TORY PETERSON

SPONSORED BY THE NATIONAL WILDLIFE FEDERATION
WASHINGTON, D. C.

The Riverside Press, Cambridge
HOUGHTON MIFFLIN COMPANY · BOSTON

OTHER BOOKS BY ROGER TORY PETERSON

A FIELD GUIDE TO THE BIRDS
Awarded the Brewster Medal
The standard book for the field identification of the birds of eastern and central North America. The indispensable "bible" of both beginners and experts. 1000 illustrations, 500 in full color.
Houghton Mifflin Company

A FIELD GUIDE TO WESTERN BIRDS
The standard western guide, using Peterson's unique Field Guide system.
Houghton Mifflin Company

BIRDS OVER AMERICA
Awarded the John Burroughs Medal
The author's adventures and his observations in his quest for birds throughout the country. Illustrated with 80 pages of his finest photographs.
Dodd, Mead and Company

THE JUNIOR BOOK OF BIRDS
For Juveniles
Houghton Mifflin Company

HOW TO KNOW THE BIRDS
An introduction to bird recognition.
Houghton Mifflin Company and New American Library

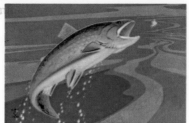

WILDLIFE IN COLOR

TEXT BY
ROGER TORY PETERSON

453 illustrations in full color by America's
leading Wildlife Artists

COLOR DESIGNS BY

WALTER WEBER	JOHN EPPENSTEINER
FRANCIS LEE JAQUES	W. C. LAWRENCE
LESLIE RAGAN	A. J. BOWMAN
ROGER TORY PETERSON	HERBERT CHRISTY
LYNN BOGUE HUNT	A. D. CUSHMAN
FRED EVERETT	RICHARD GROSSENHEIDER
FRANKLIN BOOTH	CHARLES HEXOM
MARGARET MASSON	MORGAN STINEMETZ
ELIE CHEVERLANGE	GEORGE MIKSCH SUTTON

LINE DECORATIONS BY ROGER TORY PETERSON

THE NATIONAL
WILDLIFE FEDERATION

The gallery of wildlife miniatures started in 1938 by the National Wildlife Federation has become a national institution. Each year thirty-six new paintings of birds, fish, mammals, flowers, and trees are added to this growing collection which is published as poster stamps and distributed by the Federation to support its work. The pictures in this book were painted between the years of 1939 and 1951 by some of America's finest wildlife artists. Here for the first time all of these portraits are gathered together in an integrated volume which presents the magnificent pageantry of outdoor America and tells the story of wildlife conservation.

The primary concern of the Federation is to bring to the American people a full knowledge and understanding of our natural resources. To this end it invites the efforts of all friends of the outdoors. Acting as a clearing house of information relating to conservation, it sends out news letters and clip sheets on matters of national importance, and general conservation literature. Its series of books *My Land and Your Land* is in wide use in the schools throughout the country.

National Wildlife Restoration Week, inaugurated by the Federation and established by presidential proclamation, is a special time each spring when lovers of the outdoors participate in a nationwide conservation program. It sounds the call to all people to rally to the defense of our national resources which form the basis of our national economy. Citizens are urged to guard against the overuse of soil and its erosion; the pollution of waters; and the lack of planned cutting and reforestation of our timberlands. Our lands and waters are the foundations of the national wealth; and they urgently require the active and intelligent attention of all the people.

Perhaps the most far-reaching accomplishment of the Federation has been its sponsorship of the Pittman-Robertson Act which provides that an excise tax of 10 per cent on sporting arms and ammunition shall be earmarked for allocation to the states for wildlife restoration projects and research. The passage of this law, made possible only by an overwhelming expression of favorable public opinion, is one of the greatest breaks our wildlife has ever had. Recently, a similar bill, the Dingell-Johnson Bill, which will do the same for fish, has been passed.

Alone, the individual can accomplish little. United and constant action can achieve the goal of real conservation. To that high principle the National Wildlife Federation and its many affiliated conservation-minded groups is, and has always been, uncompromisingly dedicated.

CONTENTS

WILDLIFE IN COLOR

Man, contemplating the stars, gropes for a phrase to express his awe. He contends, somewhat tritely, that he feels "very puny." However, when he turns his thoughts upon his own planet he feels, by contrast, almost like a God. He is undisputed kingpin, the dominant animal of a world in which more than 1,000,000 other species, from huge whales to minute protozoa, have been catalogued.

Yet many men go through life as though they wore horse blinders or were sleepwalking. Their eyes are open, yet they see nothing of their many wild neighbors. Their ears, attuned to motorcars and traffic, seldom detect the music of nature—the singing of birds, frogs, or crickets, or the wind in the leaves. These men, biologically illiterate, often fancy themselves well informed, perhaps sophisticated. They know business trends, or politics, yet haven't the faintest idea of "what makes the world go round."

Thumb through the pages of this book and you will find a good visual cross-section of American wildlife. How can any one claim to have "seen life" if he has ignored such prodigal variety? A flight of geese, flowers in a mountain meadow, a scarlet tanager in an oak tree, a deer by the riverbank—these are America. They are, in a sense, more truly American than our cities which, it can be argued, have their roots in the Old World.

During the first two or three centuries after Columbus made his landfall on this side of the Atlantic, the wildlife of North America changed little. By 1850, when Audubon was still alive, the human population of the United States had risen to 23,000,000, yet the continent had not lost a single bird species (the great auk was an island bird). By 1950 the population rocketed to 150,000,000, a sixfold increase in a century. During that period the Labrador duck, passenger pigeon, Carolina paroquet, and heath hen left us. The ivory-billed woodpecker, Eskimo curlew, whooping crane, California condor, and some of the fur bearers were brought to the very threshold of extinction. The buffalo, pronghorned antelope, spoonbill, and the egrets had an extremely close call, but, through last-minute protection, made a comeback.

Obviously, if man multiplies as explosively during the next century, he may well destroy himself, for, as every biologist knows, no creature can ever exceed its food supply. Hamburger does not come from the butcher shop, nor milk from the dairy; they come from the land. We are becoming aware that our "road to survival" depends on a two-point program: (1) slowing down the rapid increase in human populations which are now in such a desperate race against their own food supply; and (2) conservation—taking good care of the earth "from which all blessings flow." Wildlife, essential to healthy land, should be a part of every conservation program.

Now that no frontiers remain, and our country is settled from coast to coast, many more people than ever before are turning to nature, some for pleasure and relaxation, others to satisfy their curiosity. More than 30,000,000 visitors throng the National Parks each year. Twelve million sportsmen buy hunting licenses, 15,000,000 go fishing; not because they need meat for the table, but to get away from the nerve-racking confusion of the city, to think long thoughts, and to get closer to the things of the earth. Millions more, we do not know how many, because they do not require licenses, watch birds, or indulge in a score of other nature hobbies. Each year more than half a million people in a hundred and forty cities attend "Screen Tours," to enjoy kodachrome movies of wildlife. Bookstores report a land-office business in outdoor books. Whereas John James Audubon in his time was a puzzle to many of his friends, today it is the man who does not have some special interest in the outdoors who seems out of step.

Even though the interest in nature has had a meteoric rise in America during the last twenty or thirty years, we are still a generation behind some of the countries of northern Europe—England, the Netherlands, and Sweden, for example—in per capita interest. Ever since the days of Gilbert White of Selborne, more than a century and a half ago, birds and other wild things have been an important part of a liberal education in England. There wildlife always makes news and no important newspaper or magazine dares ignore that fact. In Sweden with but six and a half million inhabitants, less than the population of New York City, the number of outdoor books that one sees in the bookstore windows is astonishing. The Swedes love their great birch and evergreen forests, blue lakes and lonely archipelagos, and spend long holidays there. Many a schoolboy can give you not only the Swedish names of the birds and plants but the Latin names as well (after all, it was their famed Linnæus who devised the system of scientific nomenclature). However, America is not a nation to be eclipsed, and we too are rapidly becoming wildlife conscious.

Outdoor America is magnificent. We share our land with fascinating wildlife neighbors, yet the five big mediums of public enlightenment—motion pictures, radio, television, national magazines and newspapers—do not give wild things the play that they should. We can change this if we drop a card to the editor each time he runs a story we like or if we ask our local theater to feature such films as Walt Disney's *Beaver Valley* or *Seal Island*.

The man who is curious about the wild things or the growing things is never alone in his travels. To him no ocean, desert, or mountaintop is desolate. There is always life, new discoveries to be made. If he can attach names to the things he sees, so much the better. To act as a short cut to recognition so that the amateur can more quickly move on to wider horizons the Houghton Mifflin Field Guides were initiated; first the bird guides (*A Field Guide to the Birds* and *A Field Guide to Western Birds*), later those on shells, butterflies, and mammals, to be followed by field guides to trees, flowers, minerals, reptiles, and amphibians. Recognition, however, is only the first step, though a very important one, which cannot be skipped. Then, if a person is thoughtful, he may become interested in the way things live, their habits, their ecology, populations, migrations, and cycles. The best single volume summarizing these things for the whole of the animal and plant kingdoms is Dr. E. Laurence Palmer's *Fieldbook of Natural History*. It is an encyclopedia of sound information.

One cannot reflect on the forces

Aspen

Blue-winged Teal

9

which make the outdoor world tick without becoming somewhat of a conservationist. Most of us do sooner or later. This little book, while pointing out the endless variety of living things which populate America, attempts to brief the reader on some of the principles of conservation held important by those who devote their lives to wildlife research. The experts all agree that first and foremost in importance to wild creatures is their environment, a proper place to live.

Because wildlife is worth so many billions, yes *billions*, we can no longer ignore its wise use and management. This does not mean just "protection"—putting up fences and all that. Absolute protection is important when a creature is way down, the way the egret was a generation ago, but unless it has a suitable place to live all the protection in the world will do no good. It will die out regardless, as the ivory-billed woodpecker, which has very specialized needs, is doing. So wildlife conservation today involves *proper use of the land*. It is significant that every one of the standard practices of the U.S. Soil Conservation Service — strip planting, hedgerows, gully-checking, windbreaks, farm ponds—helps wildlife. Land so worn out that it will not support people, will seldom support rabbits, quail, or other wildlife either.

The three basic needs of wild creatures are food, cover and water. To increase wildlife these must be built up. But beyond a certain point the number of grouse or robins on a parcel of land cannot be increased. Each acre has its limit. You see, most birds and mammals have "territories." As I wrote in *Birds Over America*: "People are often puzzled about the robins that flutter against their reflections in dark windows. These foolish birds are not prompted by vanity; they mistake their reflection for that of another robin and are bent on chasing it away. Each male robin is a property owner. By holding territory, birds space themselves evenly over the land. They do not sing just for the delight of singing but to announce to the world their property rights. Song is not only an invitation to a prospective bride, but also a challenge to a rival. The owner is nearly invincible in his home territory. Birds, then, limit their own numbers in an area. The extra birds wander around and are chased from place to place. They form a floating population. If something happens to one of the established males, his place, his land, perhaps his wife too, are taken over by one of the "floaters." Nature, like a bank, keeps a surplus to take care of losses.

In the game species it is this "removable surplus" that might be taken by sportsmen each year. That is the point of view of the U.S. Fish and Wildlife Service and the state game commissions who attempt to peg the bag limits so that the hunting season will reap only the "interest" accrued during the year and not eat into "capital."

In somewhat this same light should *predation* (the eating of one animal by another) be viewed. Wildlife conservation does not mean destroying every kingfisher that takes a fish, or every owl that catches a rabbit. The reaction of the true sportsmen to the owl should be one of admiration for a fellow hunter—he doesn't cuss "that bloodthirsty so-and-so!" Predators have lived for millenniums in adjustment with the creatures they hunt. They never wipe out game, but take their allotted percentage, culling out the less wary or the sick. Predators are important to the natural balance, guardians as it were of the health and vigor of wildlife. Modern wildlife technicians mistrust the man who speaks heatedly of "varmints." He knows little of the biological basis of conservation. True, there are occasions when it seems necessary to control a species, but this should be done only by the proper authorities after careful study.

The pictures in this book, more than four hundred and fifty, were painted by leading wildlife artists for the National Wildlife Federation between the years of 1939 and 1951. They are arranged not by family relationships, in the traditional manner of nature books, but by wildlife communities.

This rather new way of studying animals and plants in relation to their environment is called *ecology*. There was a time when a member of a bird club looked just at birds and felt a bit guilty if he picked a strange plant or took notice of a frog. Now most of the field-glass fraternity are good all-round naturalists. Recently garden-club women have become as interested in the birds that come to their gardens as they are in their delphiniums. Sportsmen and fishermen find, in the incidental wildlife which they see and enjoy, values far beyond that of their bag. Even the Boy Scout organization no longer is satisfied with giving merit badges for Bird Study, Insect Study, etc., but is initiating more inclusive ones for Water Life, Forest Life, and Marsh Life.

To sum it up, we are becoming aware that our world is "one world," where everything is interdependent—soil, robins, and hickory trees—brook trout, damsel flies, and mink—prairies, coyotes, rivers—and men.

Black Fox

Glacier Bear

Cinnamon Bear

11

EXTINCT

No one will ever see a living mammoth. Even though carcasses have been found with flesh and hide intact, preserved by the Arctic "deep-freeze,"* the big elephant-like mammal is gone. There is no return from the black void of extinction.

We forget that thousands of species of mammals and birds became extinct before civilized man was on hand to record them; many more, in fact, than the total species living on earth today. This does not mean that they all lived contemporarily; in our dynamic world things are slowly changing and new forms are evolving. When the climate gradually alters the face of the land, dries it up or sends down ice sheets, some of the creatures die off. Change is fatal to them. And so it was that when civilized man broke down his barriers, multiplied, and spread over the entire world, he brought changes more violent in a few hundred years than those which would have taken place in millenniums.

During the last century, North America has lost at least five birds. The last great auk, a flightless, penguin-like sea bird that migrated along our coast by swimming, was recorded at Eldey Island off the coast of Iceland in 1844. A few might have survived a decade longer (one was said to have been picked up dead at Trinity Bay, Newfoundland, in 1853) but at any rate, this fabulous bird, the "garefowl" of the North Atlantic, has been gone for a century. The handsome black and

* Portions of a young mammoth are on display at the American Museum in New York City.

Mammoth

Passenger Pigeon

12

white Labrador duck was no longer seen after 1875. No one knows just why it disappeared. The passenger pigeon, now extinct, may have outnumbered *all* other birds in the United States. Skies were darkened for days by their endless flocks; huge limbs of trees were broken when they alighted. Eye-witness accounts of their great roosts read like the tales of a romancer. According to one authority, there were probably *five billion* in Audubon's day in the three states of Kentucky, Ohio, and Indiana alone. Just one century later, on September 1, 1914, the last survivor of these astronomical hordes died in the Cincinnati Zoo. The Carolina paroquet, the only parrot of our southeastern states, soon followed it. The last flock was seen in Florida in 1920. The heath hen, a race of the prairie chicken, which lived in the coastal pine barrens, survived until 1931 when the last male succumbed on Martha's Vineyard.

Mammals which have checked out since the white man came are the giant sea mink, eastern bison, eastern elk, a dozen races of the grizzly bear, and a number of others, mostly local subspecies. Fish, plants, and even butterflies have disappeared in historic times.

Islands are more vulnerable than continents. When an island is invaded by man and his followers—rats, cats, dogs, goats, the mongoose, and introduced birds with their diseases—there is no place for the native wildlife to retreat. The West Indies have lost at least fourteen birds, while the islands in the Pacific have bid aloha to *at least* one hundred—perhaps many more. How many more we don't know, for the process is going on with appalling speed.

Carolina Paroquet

Labrador Duck

Heath Hen

Whooping Crane

Nene Goose

VANISHING

Make no mistake; we must hold the line and take care of what we have left. In the nineteen-twenties one museum man insisted that the whooping crane was doomed; therefore it would be better to collect the few remaining birds and put their skins in museums for posterity! Nearly thirty years have passed, yet the whooping crane is still with us. Although agents of the National Audubon Society and the U.S. Fish and Wildlife Service have combed Arctic Canada in vain for their unknown nesting ground, the surviving cranes return each year to their winter home on the Texas coast. Thirty-six were counted in the fall of 1949—three more than there were the year before. Thirty-two were present for the roll call at the end of 1950. It is touch and go for these aristocratic white waders.

At the beginning of the century everyone thought the egrets were on the way out. Only a few colonies had escaped the plume scouts of the millinery trade. By the time the carnage was stopped there remained but a few hundred birds in remote southern swamps. Today when one drives across the Tamiami Trail in Florida or through Everglades National Park he might see thousands of these graceful white herons; little snowy egrets with "golden slippers" and big American egrets with golden bills. The big egret now even visits New England ponds and the shores of the Great Lakes each summer, and nesting colonies have become established as far north as New Jersey and Lake Erie. This dramatic example is proof that conservation is not just a theory; it works.

The rarest North American bird

Trumpeter Swan

Ivory-billed Woodpecker

(perhaps the world's rarest) is certainly the ivory-billed woodpecker. Some biologists have even questioned whether it is still with us. I watched two females near John's Bayou on the Singer Tract in Louisiana in 1942 and one female was seen there as late as March, 1947. There have been several rumors of ivory-bills since, mostly from Florida, and one confirmed report of a pair living in the northeastern part of that state in 1950. Larger than a pileated woodpecker or a crow, this magnificent species with the jaunty topknot and white bill lived in the primeval wilderness along southern rivers and disappeared when the ancient timber was cut. It simply couldn't adapt to second-growth trees. The Eskimo curlew, a large shorebird with a curved bill, is perhaps nearly as close to the lethal threshold as the ivory-bill. Although, for a while, it was thought to be extinct, a specimen reached a museum in 1932 and several have been seen since. Its problem was not one of adaptation but of persecution. Wagonloads were slaughtered when the flocks were in passage between the Arctic and the Argentine, and this once abundant species was quite spent before the era of modern game laws came in.

The California condor, America's third rarest bird, still holds on to life in certain wild canyons and ridges in southern California. There are now believed to be about sixty of these wide-winged giants left. Today even bird watchers and photographers are excluded from their mountain fortress. Still at the danger point, another western bird, the trumpeter swan, is now slowly increasing. Several hundred live on lakes in Yellowstone Park, Idaho, and British Columbia. Size is a handicap. The whooping crane is the tallest American bird, the condor has the greatest wingspan (9½ feet), and the trumpeter swan is the heaviest.

Island wildlife, as noted before, vanishes fastest. Our Hawaiian Islands have lost between half and two-thirds of their original avifauna, strange and lovely birds that lived nowhere except on these Pacific islands. The Hawaiian goose or nene (lower left) is now one of the rarest birds on earth. In 1950 only two dozen were known to exist, eighteen of which were in captivity. Perhaps as few as five wild birds still frequented the high volcanic slopes. Recently the Pacific War Memorial was created to preserve the rare and unique wildlife that still exists on some of the scattered islands of the biggest ocean.

15

Golden Pheasant

Ring-necked Pheasant

STRANGERS FROM OTHER LANDS

Some contend we have gained a bird for every one we have lost. We have lost the passenger pigeon and gained the rock dove (domestic pigeon). The heath hen is extinct, but now we have the ring-necked pheasant. The trumpeter swan has disappeared from most of its former range, but the mute or park swan of Europe has established itself locally on our soil. How desirable are these strangers? The pheasant and the mute swan are good additions, most men would agree, but the house sparrow and the starling are not. Aggressive, they are hard on bluebirds, martins, woodpeckers, and other native hole-nesting birds. However, there is nothing we can do about them now; they are here to stay.

Hundreds of thousands, perhaps millions of birds have been brought from the other continents of the world and set free in America. Years ago organizations called "acclimatization societies" were formed just for that purpose. At least 100 species were tried, from tiny songbirds to flamingos, but most of them soon died off. It is difficult to duplicate in our land the exact *habitat* or niche in which the bird lived

across the sea. The house sparrow and the starling spread like wildfire because they are city birds; a city is a city the world over. So is a farm. Almost all of our pests; the Norway rat, house mouse, cabbage butterfly, gypsy moth, brown-tail moth, Japanese beetle, ragweed, dandelion, orange hawkweed, burdock, and scores of other weeds came originally from the cities and farms of the Old World.

Many exotics were brought in accidentally. Some of our roadside flowers made their first appearance near seaports or in the ballast along railroad tracks. One attractive little butterfly that now brightens the fields in the southwest came to this country years ago as a stowaway in fodder accompanying a shipment of camels to Arizona. The nutria, a muskrat-like mammal from South America which is now profitably trapped for its fur in the marshes of Louisiana, first got its toehold, it is said, when a hurricane wrecked the cages in which a number were confined. On the other hand, no one is quite sure how the armadillo got to central Florida where it is now increasing by leaps and bounds. Perhaps

Hungarian Partridge

Chukar Partridge

someone's pet armadillos escaped.

Because there have been so many disasters when foreign plants and animals have gained a foothold, it is unlawful to bring them into our country without permission of the federal government. Most of the birds imported in recent years have been game birds. The blackcock and capercaillie of the forests of Europe have been tried many times without success. The golden pheasant and several other members of the gorgeous pheasant family have failed here because they are at home only in the wild mountain country of Asia. The ring-necked pheasant, on the other hand, a bird of the farms and paddy-fields of China, succeeded brilliantly. As many as sixteen million have been shot by sportsmen in the United States in one year—meat for the table equivalent to that of fifty thousand steers! The Hungarian partridge, a farm country bird of Europe, also does well in our prairie states.

An exception to the rule, that birds of the wilderness do not take root when transplanted, seems to be the chukar partridge from the hills of India. It is doing quite nicely on certain rocky arid slopes in the West. Perhaps it is succeeding because these hills are not already occupied by any competing native grouse or quail.

Today, before a bird or mammal is introduced, biologists make a thorough study of it in its homeland—first to make sure what its needs are, and more important, to see whether it might cause trouble to our own wildlife. It is particularly dangerous to set loose foreign creatures on islands. Many unique species are known only from single islands where they lead simple, uncomplicated lives. They cannot compete with invaders from outside.

However, it might be argued that some introductions are all to the good. There would be no frogs in Newfoundland today had not someone near the town of St. Johns missed their pleasant croaking about his home and set free some green frogs in his ponds. But surely frogs must have lived in Newfoundland before the glacial ice covered the island. So must have ruffed and spruce grouse. Neither of these grouse is there today although the spruce forests and the birch woods look just right for them. Undoubtedly these sedentary birds have not been able to get across the wide miles of the Gulf of St. Lawrence to repopulate the island since the great ice sheet moved away. To set grouse free there would be, in a sense, restocking, for they would fill a niche now empty.

NEAR HOME — THE TOWNS AND FARMS

Perhaps we shouldn't look down our noses at house sparrows, starlings, pigeons, dandelions, cabbage butterflies, and other foreign importations. They are the only wild things that many people who live in the sterile core of the big cities ever see. In the parks and suburban gardens, and on farms, nature compromises more with civilization, but even in the heart of the biggest cities, New York and Chicago, one can often find wildlife, particularly birds, for birds have wings. In downtown New York I have seen a barred owl drowsing in a tree by the City Hall, two peregrine falcons chasing the pigeons at Hearn's department store on 14th Street, a flock of migrating curlew over the rooftops of Greenwich Village, and a Virginia rail skulking in the shrubbery in a downtown public square. Most fantastic was a woodcock that had come to rest on a window ledge of

the General Motors building. Surprising numbers of migrating birds have been listed in small back yards and courts in Greenwich Village and in the "Gardens of the Nations" high above the street in Radio City. In winter ducks fly up and down the East River and the Hudson, while gulls trade back and forth between the two, giving constant life to the skyline. Central Park, an oasis of greenery in the heart of Manhattan, is a famous bird trap. Seventy-nine species of birds have been recorded there in a single May day after a weather front had stopped the night-migrating hordes over the city. Dozens of bird watchers search "The Ramble" in Central Park every morning during the month of May. Insects have wings too, so it is not surprising to hear Edwin Way Teale tell of the many small six-legged creatures he has noticed in Times Square or at the top of the Empire State building.

Some cities, like Washington, D.C., have the wilderness almost at their door. There is a bald eagle's eyrie in use within the District limits and more than once have I seen an eagle flying over downtown Washington—our national bird in our nation's capital. Turkey vultures which roost on one of the large apartment houses and warm their toes on the ventilators are sometimes mistaken for eagles. One winter a snowy owl stayed for weeks in the heart of town, harassing the flocks of starlings along Pennsylvania Avenue. One day a friend of mine discovered this owl perched like a white marble ornament on one of Washington's most beautiful marble buildings, the Shakespeare Library.

One cannot draw a precise line between the city and the farm country, because they blend, in spite of signs designating the city's official limits. Cities and towns are constantly extending their network of streets and roads. Now, three centuries after the Pilgrims landed, there are more than fifty million acres of urban lands in the United States. Farm croplands occupy more than four hundred million acres and pasture lands at least as many million more, not counting the vast open grazing range of the West. When the wilderness was pushed back, great changes came to wildlife. There was no room for the 60,000,000 buffalo or the 40,000,000 antelopes. The 2,000,000 wolves could not be tolerated and were reduced almost to the vanishing point. Some of the fur-bearers were so prized by the early trappers that they soon became very rare. On the credit side of the ledger other creatures have prospered. Deer have become very plentiful in the cut-over land in some states.

Skunks and woodchucks like the farm country, and quail find more room than they had known before the forest was broken up. Some of the songbirds benefited most of all, largely because there is more food—the seeds of weeds and the pest insects that plague the farmer.

The best kind of farm country for wildlife is where there is good *interspersion;* where the terrain is well mixed, fields broken up by woodlots, streams, hedges, and fencerows. Large windswept meadows are never as good as smaller fields separated by brushy fencerows or rows of trees. The hedges and trees help check erosion (the wearing away of the soil by wind or water) and at the same time act as "streets" by which pheasants, quail, and shy mammals can travel from place to place, without exposing themselves too much. This holds for streambanks too. Tangles and shrubs keep the banks from washing away and make the best kind of wildlife cover. A varied vista is also the most beautiful, as anyone who is familiar with the English countryside will attest. Every turn in the road presents a pleasing picture of rural loveliness—hedgerow upon hedgerow, an ancient tree left standing here and there, a stream slowly meandering through the sedge, and wildlife everywhere. By instinctively serving the cause of beauty, the English farmer has also served his land well and the wild things too. In some parts of our country we have done the same.

Naturally we make our first acquaintances near home—in the garden, or on the lawn. That is why the robin is our best-known American bird and the lowly dandelion is perhaps the most familiar flower. Our explorations begin at the doorstep.

19

American Elm

Catalpa

TREES OF THE TOWNS

A city of trees is a better city to live in. We judge the beauty of a town by its trees, but not all trees can stand the soot and smoke, the cramped root space, and the sterile soil, hard-packed between the sidewalks and the gutters. Some of the exotic trees seem to thrive best, perhaps because they had first become adapted to the teeming cities of the Old World. The ailanthus or "tree of heaven" from northern China is the most typical tree in the tiny courtyards of downtown New York City, where it is nicknamed the "Greenwich Village locust." The ginkgo, a "living fossil," which would have been extinct long ago had it not been perpetuated for many centuries in a Chinese monastery, is another favorite of city planners. Lombardy poplars, tall and plumelike, are employed to add vertical lines to landscape architecture. Planted in long rows, they look like trees on the march. Plane trees and lindens, also from Europe, and horse-chestnuts, originally from the mountains of Greece, are familiar in nearly every town. The catalpa (lower left) with its broad heart-shaped leaves and large orchid-like blossoms is really a native American, growing along the banks of some of our southern rivers. It has now been transplanted to almost every eastern town north to the Great Lakes and Boston.

The American elm (upper left), shaped like a huge flaring wineglass, is one of the finest of all street trees. Long double rows, arching over the highway until their branches interlace, give many New England towns their unique character. Elms are the favorite nesting trees of Baltimore orioles, which swing their baglike hammocks from the tips of the long branches. During the past twenty years the Dutch elm disease, caused by a fungus first discovered in the Netherlands, has destroyed countless elms from Boston west to Indiana and as far south as Virginia. Every effort is being made to control it, so that the elm will not join the ill-fated chestnut.

The architectural beauty of the city of Washington is enhanced not only by elms but by many huge sycamores, or American plane trees, with their ghostly trunks and wide spreading branches. The American species can readily be told from the European plane tree by its much whiter bark. Besides the elms and sycamores, some of the oaks, ashes, willows, hackberry, and a few other native trees are hardy enough for city planting. If you would know what shade trees to plant and how to keep them healthy send for Trees, the 1949 yearbook of the U.S. Department of Agriculture.

As our towns grow older, so will the trees. There is no reason why some of them should not eventually reach the venerable age of two or three centuries. But the lives of city trees are not their own. They must come down when streets are widened, and their branches must be trimmed when they interfere with the wires. Cavities which would make good homes for screech owls or squirrels are plugged up by tree surgeons; dead limbs are lopped off. Everything in a city is kept trimmed and orderly—the gardens, hedges, lawns, and the trees. No doubt we should have many more birds in our cities were it not for this practice of keeping everything manicured.

Lombardy Poplar

Sycamore

21

Apple Tree

TREES OF THE FARMS

Clean country air is better for trees than sooty city air. Like the rest of us, trees are healthier when they grow up on the farm. On a well-planned farm most of the trees serve some purpose. The regimented rows of peach, apple, cherry, and other fruit trees are tended as carefully as the livestock. But because spraying eliminates most of the insects, and removing dead limbs does away with nesting holes, many modern fruit groves are quite barren of birds. Abandoned orchards are really much better for wildlife. If the countryman likes birds, he will cherish a few "neglected" trees and will perhaps plant some mulberry trees for the robins and waxwings, if for no other reason than to divert them from the cherries.

Full-bodied sugar maples might be planted near the house for their shade or their beauty (they are spectacular in October), or they might be grown in the farm woodlot, to be tapped in early spring for their sweets. Feathery-leaved honey locusts are also decorative when grouped near the house. They too are sometimes grown in the woodlot where they will eventually be cut for fence-posts. Almost any tree will grow on a farm, but most are planted for "practical" reasons. The squat shrubby Osage orange, for example, makes the perfect windbreak. Throughout the open farmlands of the Midwest it is planted in long dense rows, forming thickets that incidentally provide cover for nesting robins, doves, catbirds, thrashers, song sparrows, and all the other birds which keep the surrounding croplands free of pests.

Peach Blossom

22

Sugar Maple

Honey Locust

Red Mulberry

Osage Orange

Butter-and-eggs

Evening Primrose

Wild Sunflower

FLOWERS OF THE FIELDS
AND ROADSIDE

Nearly all of the flowers that grow in vacant lots are immigrants. So are a very large percentage of those along the roadside. At least a hundred common roadside flowers—including most of our "weeds"—came from Europe. The list is long: black mustard, bouncing bet, red clover, white clover, Queen Anne's lace, spearmint, peppermint, mullein, butter-and-eggs, teasel, chicory, dandelion, devil's paintbrush, field daisy, burdock, bull thistle, and many many others. Some, like the handsome day lily of Asia escaped from gardens, but most of them came unseen, as tiny seeds mixed in with shipments from across the sea. That is why the first known station for a new stranger is often at a seaport or along a railroad track. All this confirms what has been said before, that a city or a farm is the same the world over. A house mouse, a rat, or a starling sees little difference between London and New York. Neither do the many weeds that have followed man across the Atlantic.

However, with the exception of the butter-and-eggs (upper left) an attractive visitor from Europe, the flowers shown here, and on the two pages that follow, do not fall into this category. They are as native as the red man, even though the black-eyed susan (upper right) did march eastward from the prairies when the forest was opened up. On eastern fields it met the white daisy, a traveler from abroad, and eventually returned the visit by hopping the

574 P44
c. 2

Atlantic and establishing a beachhead in Europe. There it is often planted in gardens and so are our native goldenrods.

The evening primrose has not allowed the invading army of foreign flowers to displace it. It will grow in any vacant lot, unfolding its petals toward dusk so that the moths may drink. When the hours of darkness are gone and daylight disperses the long-tongued sphinx moths and noctuids, the golden blossoms do not at once close, but remain open during the cool of morning so that the bees and butterflies may have their chance. By midday the show is over.

The milkweed (right center) repels cattle with its bitter milky juices and even the monarch butterfly, whose larvæ feed on the leaves, is left strictly alone by the birds. When butterflies or bees, seeking nectar, alight on the seductive blossoms their feet slip into the narrow slots between the waxy petals. Struggling for a better footing, the leg becomes even more deeply wedged in the slit. Finally, a sharp jerk releases the foot, but not until a tiny saddlebag of pollen has been fastened to it. In such complex fashion is cross-pollination assured. Later, when the brown seeds become ripe they take off on silken parachutes. No plant is better equipped for survival than the milkweed.

Sunflowers of at least three dozen species come into bloom in late summer and autumn. One is the state flower of Kansas. Of the goldenrods there are an even greater variety. One hundred and twenty-five kinds spread their cloth of gold across the continent, from the mountaintops to the dunes at the edge of the sea. None of this generous genus is more loved than the plume-like Canada goldenrod (lower right).

Black-eyed Susan

Common Milkweed

Canada Goldenrod

25

Wild Rose and Tiger Swallowtail

Trumpet-vine

Trumpet Honeysuckle

From May to October there is a constantly changing parade of bloom along the roadside, reaching a climax at summer's end with the goldenrods, wild sunflowers, and asters. The ideal roadside is not where "clean farming" has plowed the turf right up to the fence, but where a wide strip has been left to run wild and act as a barrier against erosion. In such hedgerows quail might hide and song sparrows may nest. There also will we find wild roses blooming in early July, each blossom lasting about two days before its frail petals drop away. Later in the season birds eat the red hips and scatter the seeds in other spots along the fence row. In that way birds and plants work for their mutual survival. Along such roads the trumpet honeysuckle (Lonicera) clambers over the shrubbery, offering its scarlet trumpets to the hummingbirds and long-tongued butterflies. Hummingbirds seem to have a preference for red flowers. The flaming flowers of the trumpet-vine (Bignonia) are another favorite of these jeweled midgets, who must probe deep if they wish to get at the nectar. In the process the hummingbird's forehead is dusted with pollen which is carried from flower to flower, assuring fertilization.

In moist, rank meadows one might look for the Canada lily whose nodding bells toll the midsummer hours. It is true that Solomon in all his glory was not arrayed as one of these. The temptation is to pick it, but whereas one may gather bouquets of daisies or asters, which replenish themselves abundantly, or may pick violets sparingly, he should leave the lilies strictly alone, to be admired where they grow. Many native flowers have almost disappeared where there is much plowing, cutting of forests, or grazing of livestock. So when you find a pocket of these scarcer plants, a glade in which they still grow, let them live. However, if the place is about to be leveled by a bulldozer you might with a clear conscience transplant them to your garden.

Sometimes in sterile sandy soil colonies of lupines grow beside the road, looking as if they had been planted and abandoned. But even though they resemble the lupines in our gardens they are quite wild. In the West, particularly in the Pacific states, lupines come in all colors; there are many of them, but in the East we have only the blue one shown here.

Asters come in a variety of shades too, particularly blues and violets. But among the 150 species of asters in the United States there are many white ones, such as the starved or calico aster pictured on the right. Incidentally, the small white asters are a confusing lot even to expert botanists, who often throw up their hands in despair when trying to identify them. No flowers are more successful in the fight for existence than the composites (the asters, daisies, goldenrods, sunflowers, etc.). They use the mass-production technique. Examine an aster or daisy closely and you will find that each yellow center is really made up of dozens of tiny flowers. The surrounding "petals" or rays merely act as showy advertisements to the insects which are so necessary to pollination.

Blooming early and hugging the ground where they almost escape notice among the long grass are several kinds of wild strawberries (lower right). The large garden strawberries are hybrids, a blend of New World and Old World varieties.

Canada Lily

Wild Lupine

Calico Aster

Wild Strawberry

27

Praying Mantis

Bumblebee and Red Clover

Dragonfly and Cattail

INSECTS OF THE ROADSIDE

The bumblebee on the clover brings to mind a famous riddle: "Why are old maids the pillars of the British Empire?" Because old maids keep cats, cats catch field mice; with fewer mice to eat the grubs of bumblebees, more bees grow up to pollinate the clover. More clover for cattle to fatten on means more beef to give strength to the fighting men of the Empire.

There is no doubt that insects are important. No one really knows how many species there are. At least 15,000 are found within a few miles of New York City. Throughout the world nearly 700,000 have been named and there might well be an equal number undescribed, perhaps a million or more. Some insects have become serious pests, increasingly so because of our intensive agricultural practices; but we are wrong in regarding them all as pests. Hundreds of birds would become extinct if they were gone. The higher plants also depend on insects; they evolved together. Flowering plants give their nectar and some of their leaves to the insects; the insects return the favor by pollinating them so there will be seeds another year. That is why na-

Monarch Butterfly

Tiger Swallowtail and Joe-pye Weed

turalists fear a wholesale use of DDT might make a biological desert of the countryside.

Insects multiply enormously, furnishing many birds and some small mammals with most of their food. As a safeguard against too great numbers, insects have *parasites*, tiny insects that bore within their eggs or larvæ, and *predators*, like the dragonfly (lower left) which hawks over the ponds for mosquitoes. The praying mantis, another predator, seizes its prey with its hooked forelegs.

Butterflies not only service the flowers, but contribute their beauty to the fields. The big milkweed butterfly, or monarch, is perhaps the most dramatic species because it migrates in almost the manner of the birds, flying south in fall, returning in spring. It has even been known to cross the Atlantic and has been recorded 157 times in Great Britain. Swallowtails—the tiger swallowtail and the various black swallowtails—are the largest and handsomest butterflies, the gay little sulphurs the most abundant. Others like the brown wood nymphs skip about the meadows almost unnoticed. If you would identify and know more about them, don't miss the new *Field Guide to the Butterflies* by Alexander Klots.

Black Swallowtail, Sulphur, and Ironweed

29

Woodchuck

Skunk

MAMMALS OF THE FARM COUNTRY

There are several ways to take a walk. You might step along at a good pace, just for the exercise, but with your thoughts elsewhere, or you might bring along a friend and talk baseball or politics. However, if you would see wildlife you will keep silent, with eyes and ears open, alert for the least movement. True, you will rarely see a fox; its nose will warn it that you are coming. But you will see a surprising number of small mammals that have settled down as neighbors in our rural economy. Some, like the skunk, are not much loved, but unless one gets into the chicken yard, which it does occasionally, it isn't a bad fellow. Over half of its diet is insects and mice, although it will eat almost anything (it just loves turtle's eggs). Because of its habits and its fur mammalogists rate the skunk as one of the most valuable wild animals. Many people know this striped night prowler only by the odor when one has been run over on the highway.

The burly woodchuck, star performer on ground-hog day, is not much appreciated either because it sometimes raids the garden, but in Pennsylvania it has been protected because its burrows give refuge to rabbits, an important game animal. It eats green things all summer long, storing up fat so that it can sleep through the long winter deep in its burrow. A woodchuck that lived near our house ate nearly all the leaves from a morning-glory vine that covered our woodpile; then for a few days consumed only giant ragweed (which pleased me, a hay-fever sufferer). Meanwhile the morning-glory sent out new leaves and became more luxuriant than before. Fortunately, the ragweed didn't do the same.

Mice of at least three or four kinds live on every farm—the pesky and not too clean house mouse, the ever-hungry meadow mouse, and the appealing white-footed mouse (upper right). The immaculate little white-foot with its large brown eyes and big translucent ears makes a much better neighbor than the other two. It will help itself to nubbins of grain in the fields, but it also eats all the grasshoppers and other insects it can lay its tiny white paws on. A dynamo, it hardly slows down even in winter when so many other mammals take their long sleep. Leaving its cozy nest inside a dead stump, or last year's vireo's nest which it has roofed over, it comes out at night to explore the white winter world. The next morning its tiny tracks are everywhere, making lacy patterns in the snow.

Chipmunks, scampering about old stone walls like nervous four-legged birds, also pack tremendous energy into a small package. Like the rest of the squirrel family they have partially accepted the pattern of civilization. Red squirrels (page 71) prefer evergreen woods, but a few make their homes in orchards and shade trees. We would appreciate these attractive little animals more if it were not for the many small birds and eggs they account for. However, when large owls are about, particularly horned owls, the squirrel population is kept within proper limits. The friendly gray squirrel, more civilized than the red, often comes uninvited to the feed tray, but it seldom bothers the nesting birds. However, in England where it was unwisely introduced it has become a real problem. All squirrels are important planters of trees. Many of the acorns which they bury would not otherwise take root.

It is astonishing that a predator like the red fox can exist in farming country, but it often does. Renegade foxes sometimes get into the hen roost, but usually these intelligent collie-like animals prefer to avoid trouble and hunt for other fare. They are probably the world's greatest mousers and are worth millions of dollars each year to fur trappers and fur farmers. Some landowners prefer to regard foxes and skunks as a crop, to be taken care of, rather than "vermin" to be exterminated.

White-footed Mouse

Eastern Chipmunk

Gray Squirrel

Red Fox

31

Purple Martin

Barn Swallow

BIRDS OF THE TOWNS AND FARMS

From my studio window, without rising from my drawing board, I can see or hear fifty kinds of birds on any summer's day, and at least twenty in winter. Yet I live within the limits of a small village, a suburb of Washington, D.C. Many songbirds have adapted their way of life to ours, have pulled up stakes and moved to town. Large gardens in the suburbs, and estates with their varied landscapes, often have a density of birds higher than one can find anywhere else except, perhaps, in a good swamp. This is because most birds like "edge"; they prefer the borders of woods, not the deep heart of the forest; the margins of fields, not the great open stretches. The settling of the land has broken up the forest and the prairies into smaller parcels. There are fewer woodpeckers, and fewer vireos, perhaps, than there were when anchors were first dropped off Plymouth; but there are undoubtedly many more song sparrows, chipping sparrows, field sparrows, cardinals, mockingbirds, catbirds, kingbirds, indigo buntings, yellow warblers, chewinks, goldfinches, and others. For this reason we believe, but of course we don't

know for certain, that the total population of songbirds is greater than it was in the days of the pilgrims.

The swallows, in particular, have been opportunists. Every member of this adaptable family has endorsed man's works and has prospered. The barn swallow (deeply forked tail) nests on the beams and rafters inside barns while the cliff swallow (buffy rump) plasters its jug-like nests under the eaves outside. The bank swallow digs its tunnels in road cuts and sand quarries, while the tree swallow and violet-green swallow (western U.S.) are pleased to build in bird boxes. The purple martin, the largest swallow, has the distinction of being the first American bird to accept bird houses, hollow gourds which the Indians hung from saplings. Today most martins live in miniature apartment houses. They are our only native birds who will tolerate other families under the same roof. In fact, they enjoy their neighbors and prefer their doorways low enough so they can look out and see what is going on while they attend to the tedious job of brooding.

I have often wondered what the original niche of the Baltimore oriole was when George Calvert, the first Lord Baltimore, found it along the Chesapeake. Today it is a town bird, darting like a bright flame through the green elm trees that line the village streets. If the Dutch elm disease takes away most of our elms, what will the orioles do then? Will they find some other tree a good substitute?

Mourning doves seldom venture far into town, but every farm has its quota. If we were to take a summer trip from New York across the plains to the Pacific and back by way of the South, we should probably see these small wild doves on every day of our journey.

The robin, perhaps the best-loved American bird, and certainly the best known, has completely forsaken the wilderness in the East. Today it is a dooryard bird. In the far West, however, the robin still prefers the yellow pine forests of the mountains and in parts of Canada it clings to an uncivilized existence in the wild spruce country.

The sleek crested cedar waxwings with waxy red tips on their wing feathers are also familiar on farms from coast to coast. If a mulberry tree is in fruit, a flock will be sure to be there, and perhaps a half-dozen other kinds of birds too.

With such prodigal variety almost at the dooryard is it any wonder that bird-watching is fast becoming a favorite hobby? Springtime, naturally, is when most people suddenly become bird conscious, but as a matter of fact, there is not a month in the year when things are not happening. Winter or early spring is the best time for the beginner to start. The only equipment needed to join in the fun is a good field guide and a pair of binoculars.

Baltimore Oriole

Mourning Dove

Robin

Cedar Waxwing

33

Screech Owl

Barn Owl

The two birds above are flying mousetraps. Mice abound on most farms, and were it not for the owls, hawks, weasels, skunks, and foxes, the destructive little rodents would cause far more damage than they do. Screech owls can be either red or gray; it has nothing to do with their age or sex. A red one might even be mated to a gray one, but no matter what its color, a screech owl can always be identified by its ear tufts. It is the only small owl with these ornaments (except in parts of the Southwest where the spotted and flammulated screech owls are found).

Whereas the little screech owl prefers to live in the apple orchard or among the shade trees, the barn owl, or "monkey-faced" owl, is the owl of the buildings. In Europe it haunts ancient castles and ruins. In America, it sometimes enters cities as large as Washington and New York, where it secretly raises a family of golliwogs in some abandoned tower or church belfry. A tower in the old Smithsonian building in Washington has been occupied continuously by barn owls for more than eighty years. At dusk, you may see them as they fly forth over the government buildings to hunt rats and mice or, in winter, the starlings that crowd the long ledges.

The red-headed woodpecker, which Audubon proclaimed one of the most beautiful of all American birds, likes the semi-open rural country with its farm groves and telegraph poles. Lately it has become quite scarce in many states where it once was common. Motorcars are one of its chief hazards because it has the fatal habit of flying from a fencepost when a car approaches and swooping low across the road. In some states more redheads are killed by traffic than any other bird. Now the starling from Europe is driving it from its holes. We earnestly hope we won't lose the redhead.

At least fifty species of North American birds have been known to nest in bird boxes. Most of these are birds that normally build their nests in abandoned woodpecker holes or decayed hollows in old trees. The house wren, for example, used to nest in second-hand downy-woodpecker holes in the swampy woods along the creeks. It still does sometimes, but now it prefers to live in town, for nearly everyone puts up boxes for wrens.

In putting up bird houses remember these "Don'ts": (1) Do not make a box "for birds," but for a specific kind of bird, a bluebird, a swallow, or a wren; (2) do not make the hole too large (house wren, diameter 1 inch, bluebird, 1½ inches); (3) do not make the hole near the bottom of the box except in martin houses; (4) do not build boxes with more than one room, except for martins, because most birds are territorial; (5) do not use tin cans or metal—they heat up in the sun; (6) do not put up too many boxes in an area; (7) do not leave last year's nests in the boxes. If you wish to build bird houses or would like to know how to make your garden more attractive to birds read the *Handbook of Attracting Birds* by Thomas P. McElroy, Jr., or the *Picture Primer of Attracting Birds* by Russell Mason.

Nearly everyone seems to have wrens in mind when they put up boxes, but bluebirds need them more. These gentle birds have been pushed around by the invading starlings which take over their nesting sites. Their soft voices are now not heard as often in some farm areas and they have taken to nesting in mailboxes for want of better accommodations. They need encouragement. Boxes nailed to the south side of fenceposts, three or four feet from the ground, will suit them perfectly, but will not appeal so much to starlings or sparrows.

Hummingbirds can be attracted to the garden by putting out vials of sugar water wrapped in bright red ribbon. Out of a family of 320 tropical species the tiny ruby-throat, which weighs less than a copper penny, is the only one adventurous enough to make the 500-mile flight across the Gulf of Mexico to the eastern United States. The western states are more blessed with hummers. They have a dozen species. One, the rufous hummingbird, travels as far as Alaska.

Red-headed Woodpecker

House Wren

Ruby-throated Hummingbird

Eastern Bluebird

35

Killdeer

Upland Plover

BIRDS OF THE FIELDS

How many birds per acre are there on a farm? Some years ago, the U.S. Department of Agriculture made a survey of farms throughout the United States and found that they averaged two and a quarter birds per acre. That was before soil conservation was practiced as widely as it is now. Today well-managed farms which include wildlife in their plans often support two or three times that many.

Quail, pheasants, bobolinks, meadowlarks, and other birds that nest in the hay fields have serious trouble if the hay is mowed too early. Many of them are cut to pieces by the sharp blades while sitting tight on their eggs. Flushing bars, a device that sweeps the grass ahead of the knife blades and causes the birds to fly, saves many lives. They should be a standard part of all mowing machinery.

The noisy, good-looking killdeer belongs to the plowed fields and pastures where the grass has been grazed short. The two rings across its breast and the rusty tail are its marks. Those who know the habits of killdeers are not misled by the spectacular drooping-wing trick when the bird pretends injury (see above). Instead, they search for the nest —a scrape with four spotted pear-shaped eggs which look almost like the naked pebbles on which they lie.

The upland plover (not a plover but a sandpiper) is a long-distance champion which travels to Argentina. We hear its mellow kip-ip-ip-ip high in the air on nights in August when it is on the first leg of its long journey. Because for years it was a restaurant delicacy in South America it is not nearly so plentiful in our midwestern fields as it was when grandfather was a boy. Its song is one of the weirdest, wildest sounds in nature, two long-drawn wind-like whistles: whoooooleeeeeeeee, wheeeelooooooooooo.

The bobolink, master musician of the daisy fields, makes a similar journey to the pampas of the Argentine and back every year, a trip that might cover more than 7000 miles each way. The spring flocks come in from the Caribbean with a rush. They do not loiter but press on impatiently, the males singing in wild chorus as they go. Whether a bobolink spends the summer in Maine or across the continent in British Columbia, it usually enters and leaves the United States via Florida. The ecstatic aerial performance of the bobolink might be called an "advertising song." Many birds of the meadows and the prairies have this type of song which they pour forth while fluttering high in the air; it is their way of calling attention to themselves in the wide open spaces. The skylark of Europe is the classic example. Our horned lark has such a song and so has the upland plover.

The dickcissel, which looks like a little sparrow-sized meadowlark, has moved away from the Atlantic seaboard within historic times and is now seldom seen east of the Appalachians. Its staccato dick-ciss-ciss-ciss is a familiar sound all through the alfalfa fields of the Midwest.

The chunky meadowlark can be identified by its white outer tail feathers when it flies, or by the black V on its breast, if it doesn't turn its back on you when you focus the binoculars. It really belongs to the blackbird family, but the horned lark (lower right) is a true lark, blood brother to the European skylark. Whereas the meadowlark and bobolink like their grass long and lush, the horned lark prefers it short and sparse, with bald spots. Although in the East it often favors golf courses it is really a bird of the open range, outnumbering all other birds combined on our vast western plains. There must be many millions of them.

The meadow birds shown on these two pages are not all of them; there are others—the vesper sparrow, grasshopper sparrow, savannah sparrow, and others, not to mention the swallows, crows, starlings, blackbirds, and mourning doves that use the fields as a happy hunting ground.

Bobolink

Dickcissel

Meadowlark

Prairie Horned Lark

37

Woodcock

Song Sparrow

White-throated Sparrow

Yellow-breasted Chat

BIRDS OF
THE BRUSHY PLACES

When a field is abandoned, weeds take over, then small bushes sprout here and there. The bobolinks and meadowlarks may hold on for awhile, but sooner or later give up their home to newcomers, song sparrows and field sparrows. Pheasants and quail now find the cover better than it was when the field was an unbroken stretch of grass. As the shrubs grow and vines clamber over them, catbirds, towhees, and chats come in. Some of the song sparrows and field sparrows must then go elsewhere. Eventually, saplings will reach for the light and redstarts and vireos will sing. In due time (long after we are gone) the second-growth trees will become a climax forest. We call this chain of events *succession*, an important word in our wildlife vocabulary. The brushy places are a partway stage in succession between the field and the forest.

The woodcock, that droll-looking game bird which haunts the damp thickets, has a spectacular flight song, believe it or not. At dusk on spring nights in some bog or pasture it can be heard grunting its deep nasal *beezp*. Flying up suddenly it mounts in a broad spiral toward the moon, its wings chippering musically, then high in the air it bursts into an inspired bubble-pipe-like warble and plunges back to earth. Many bird watchers make special trips on May evenings to hear this performance. If it is not too dark they might even see the dim silhouette of the bird against the sky.

Sparrows abound in the thickets. Song sparrows with streaked breasts build their nests there and give us constant pleasure with their singing. White-throated sparrows from the cool woodlands of New England and Canada stop in migration and timidly whistle their thin icy notes. They might even spend the winter in company with the ubiquitous song sparrows if it is not too far north.

The yellow-breasted chat, a summer dweller in the brushy places, acts the part of clown, acrobat, and ventriloquist. Odd clucks, caws, mews, and whistles issue from the tangles while the chat itself remains hidden. Then, unable to restrain itself longer, it flings itself into the air, singing wildly, and parachutes back with flopping wings and dangling legs. It is classified by systematists as a warbler, but it is half again as large as any of the others of that tribe, with more the loose-jointed personality of the mimic thrushes (catbird, thrasher, and mockingbird) with which it shares the thickets.

Towhees (page 62) are also typical birds of the slashings. So are goldfinches (upper right) and the yellow-billed cuckoo, although they can be found in orchards and woodlands as well.

One of the most numerous birds of the brushy places in some parts of the East and Midwest is the gorgeous little indigo bunting. In the Appalachians it inhabits every burn and roadside slashing where the shrubs are not too high. While driving through the hills on hot midsummer days one may hear its penetrating song more constantly than that of any other bird. The blue grosbeak with which it is sometimes confused is decidedly larger with tan wing bars and a larger bill. More southern than the indigo bird, it seems nowhere very common.

Goldfinch

Yellow-billed Cuckoo

Indigo Bunting

Blue Grosbeak

THE DECIDUOUS WOODLANDS

A squirrel, in primeval days, might have leapt from bough to bough for a thousand miles, so continuous were the forests. The first settlers thought that the entire continent was probably cloaked in a luxuriant green mantle of trees, but when men pushed westward they found that only half of it was so covered. West of the Mississippi, trees gave way to seas of grass, the great divide which separates the eastern hardwood forest from the evergreen-covered Rockies.

The U.S. Department of Agriculture states precisely that there are 1182 species of forest trees in the United States. At least half of them grow in the Southeast, particularly in the Appalachians. This region, probably as rich in variety as any in the world, can claim twice as many species as the whole continent of Europe.

We divide the trees into two main categories; the *evergreens* or *coniferous*

trees, which have narrow needles and cones, and the *deciduous* trees, those with broad flat leaves which usually fall at the approach of winter. The states east of the plains are clothed primarily by deciduous trees. Conifers dominate the endless forests which spread across Canada. Conifers also predominate in the vast uplands of our western mountains.

Few trees which offered their shade to the first settlers still stand. Fortunately, a few virgin groves in the East have been spared, giving us some picture of the forest primeval, where forest giants with immense boles tower above their neighbors. These very old trees do not crowd in dense ranks but stand apart with smaller trees and shrubs between. In places the sunlight even reaches the ground. Such a wilderness might be likened to a city—there are young trees, old trees, seedlings being born, saplings growing up, trees dying.

Silviculturists like to think of a stand of timber in this way—as a balanced community—and consider it unwise to level a woodlot at a sweep. They believe it better to crop trees selectively, taking some, leaving others to mature for harvesting at a later date. Or they advocate clean-cutting patches of trees at a time, not the entire forest. Either method of management results in a healthy balance, good for birds and the other wild things, which like the open spots or edges, rather than the unbroken stretches of forest.

How dull is the woodlot which had been leveled thirty or forty years before, where all the second-growth trees are of the same age, crowded together, forming a closed canopy which completely excludes the sunlight! A few red-eyed vireos might be in the branches above, and ovenbirds in the shadows beneath, but little else. Such a woodlot is vulnerable. Because there are few birds on hand to eat the insects an epidemic of tent caterpillars might sweep through, or brown-tailed moths, webworms, or some other pest. Denuded of leaves many of the naked trees may die. Or some year not enough rain may fall, so some of the overcrowded trees perish of thirst. In this way, by opening up breathing spaces in the forest, nature corrects things. New growth is given a chance.

Naturalists often use the word "edge" to describe borderline environments. It might mean the edge of the woods, an open spot in the woods, a brushy roadside, the edge of a meadow or margin of a swamp. At the edge of a woodlot there might be everything from grass to grown trees. Flowers and shrubs are often massed along the margin in a terrace effect that would do

credit to a skilled landscape architect. There one always finds the most birds. "Edge" is very important to wildlife. It is the point of transition, where competition is keenest.

Some years forest fires burn as much as 36,000,000 acres in the United States. This is an area larger than New York State, or as large as all New England excluding Connecticut. This may represent as many as two hundred thousand separate conflagrations. Most are small brush fires, easily put out, but some sweep thousands of acres. One of the most disastrous fires of all time was the one which wiped out Peshtigo, Wisconsin, in 1871. Over 1,280,000 acres were swept by roaring flames. Fifteen hundred people were burnt alive, over seven times as many as lost their lives in the historic Chicago fire, which happened on the very same day.

What causes these fires? The U.S. Forest Service tells us that many are started by campers who neglect to put out their campfires, smokers who carelessly toss down cigarette butts or matches, and by arsonists who deliberately set the fires for twisted reasons of their own. Statistics show that at least two-thirds of the fires could have been prevented!

Good forestry keeps wildlife in mind. Protection from fire helps a lot. So does protection from grazing—keeping out the sheep and cattle which eat down the seedlings, small shrubs, and ground cover. Some cutting of the trees, and opening up of the woods, can even raise the wildlife crop. Birds and mammals like the open glades and sunny spots. A few dead trees for the hole-nesting birds should be left and so should large den trees where raccoons, possums, and squirrels can live.

41

Red Oak

White Hickory

Black Walnut

White Ash

TREES OF THE WOODLANDS

Some trees bear nuts, some winged seeds, others berries or fruits. Wildlife can take its pick. Squirrels and jays unwittingly become foresters when they bury acorns and forget where they hid them. Some of these acorns sprout and become great oaks like the red oak at the upper left. The red oak (red in autumn glory only) is widespread east of the plains. Hickories are strictly American trees, loved by both boys and squirrels. The white hickory, the hickory of the hilltops, does not have as tasty kernels as the shagbark or some of the others. They are rather bitter, but not too bad. The black walnut, on the other hand, bears one of the most delicious of all nuts, reserved for fine cookies and candies. Growing in rich woodlands, the tree might reach a height of 150 feet. The beech, the lovely silvery-trunked tree on which sweethearts carve their initials, brings forth a great crop of three-cornered nutlets some years. In bygone days passenger pigeons used to fatten on them.

Those of us who are old enough remember wistfully when we used to go forth in the fall to gather chestnuts. A blight first noticed in New York City in 1904 has destroyed virtually all the chestnut trees from Canada to the Gulf states. No greater catastrophe has ever befallen a tree in our times.

The white ash and the other ashes have winged seeds, eaten by some of the finches. Straight-trunked, they are found scattered throughout the forest, not in "pure stands" as beech trees often are.

The coffee-tree of the Mississippi Valley has but one close relative, and

Chestnut

Beech

Coffee-tree

Tulip-tree

that lives in southern China. Usually a lonely, solitary tree, its leaves come forth late and drop early, leaving it quite naked for more than six months of the year, like a dead thing. The seed pods are very large, six to ten inches long, containing large, dark seeds from which old settlers made a coffee-like drink.

Throughout the valleys of the eastern states and the lower Mississippi belt the straight upright trunks of tulip-trees support masses of glossy-green leaves which are somewhat tulip-like in outline. Actually it is the cuplike greenish-yellow and orange blossoms which give the tree its name.

The little redbud or "Judas tree" with its heart-shaped leaves goes almost unnoticed most of the year, but in early spring before the leaves appear it sets the countryside ablaze with a spectacular show of bright pink blossoms.

The persimmon, most northerly

member of the ebony group, is typical of the southern and central states. Although neither deer nor cattle will browse its unpalatable leaves the round fruits are a favorite of possums and other wild creatures after a frost has sweetened them. As any country boy knows, they are puckering and astringent if not fully ripe.

The American linden or basswood, another tree with heart-shaped leaves, is one of the more important forest trees of the Appalachian belt and the central states. It is estimated that nine billion board feet grow in the United States.

When the forest takes over, the red cedar dies out. It prefers abandoned fields and dry slopes, but often grows in swamps too. There the dark pyramids give an ornamental touch to the landscape. They offer their bluish berries to the birds and protect them against winter winds.

Redbud

Persimmon

American Linden

Red Cedar

Yellow Trout-lily

White Trillium

SPRING FLOWERS
OF THE WOODLANDS

The annual parade of flowers begins in the woods. It ends in the open country, in the meadows and along the roadsides. The early spring flowers shown here burst from the leaf mold and unfold their delicate petals soon after the last snows melt, before the new leaves of the trees overhead shut out the sunlight. But go into the same woodland in summer; you will find very few flowers there then. There are, of course, some at the edges of the woods and in the clearings but almost none in the shady depths where the hepaticas and spring beauties lifted their faces in April.

Most spring flowers are easy to identify. True, some of the blue violets are difficult, but most flowers are not. However, as summer progresses the problem of recognition becomes harder and harder until, by autumn, the welter of goldenrods and asters causes many an experienced botanist to sigh hopelessly. To complicate things, many of the composites hybridize.

The trout-lily, or adder's tongue (upper left), has mottled leaves and nodding yellow blossoms. The trilliums have all their parts in threes (three leaves, three petals, three sepals, etc.). The white trillium, the largest kind, turns pink when fading. Bloodroot is named for the red bloody juices which ooze from its stem when picked; Dutchman's breeches is named for the shape of its blossoms. Trailing arbutus opens its small pink blossoms under the oaks and pines soon after the earth thaws. Hepaticas might be white, blue-

46

Bloodroot

Dutchman's Breeches

Trailing Arbutus

Round-lobed Hepatica

Big Merrybell

Bird's-foot Violet

lavender, or pink. Their three-lobed leaves are their badge of identity.

Nearly eighty species of wild violets grow in North America. Some are white, some yellow, but most are varying shades of blue or blue-purple. It takes a trained botanist to run down some of the blue ones, but there are others which can be identified at a glance. Such a one is the bird's-foot violet with its bicolored blossoms and deeply cleft leaves. Violets, probably more than any other spring flowers, have inspired a love of wildflowers in children. They may be picked sparingly.

There are three or four kinds of bellworts or "merrybells" in the spring woodlands, but the handsomest is the one shown here, big merrybells. The yellow blossom with its half-twisted petals droops like a flower just past its bloom, or one just coming into bloom. During April and May it might be found in rich calcareous woods from Quebec to Georgia.

Jack-in-the-pulpit belongs to the same family as the homely skunk cabbage and the immaculate calla lily, the arums. The striped hood forms a canopied pulpit for "Jack," the flowering stalk inside.

Dr. Paul Bartsch once told a group

that if they listened intently they might hear Jack speak. One of the ladies knelt down, listened, then said skeptically that she could hear nothing.

"Don't you?" asked Dr. Bartsch. "It is very distinct."

"What does he say," inquired the woman.

With a twinkle in his eye Dr. Bartsch replied, "Enjoy us, but don't destroy us."

This has since become a slogan of the Wild Flower Preservation Society.

Perhaps no flowers need protection more than our native orchids. Should you find one of these shy treasures, get down on your hands and knees and admire it where it grows. Most people think of orchids as a strictly tropical group, but we have 140 species in North America. Some are insignificant greenish sprouts, hardly more impressive than a sprig of asparagus. Others, like the lady's slippers, are almost as flamboyant as some of the hothouse products.

The yellow lady's slipper grows among the ferns of rich woodlands from Newfoundland to the mountains of Georgia, blossoming during May and June. Its lower petal is like a waxen slipper, while the upper ones suggest twisted ribbons or unfastened shoe-

Jack-in-the-Pulpit

Yellow Lady's Slipper

strings. "Whip-poor-will's shoe" is a very appropriate nickname for it. For a similar reason, the pink lady's slipper (right center) has been named the "moccasin flower." It prefers drier, more acid woodlands, but it can also be found in bogs or wet woods, particularly further north. It is sometimes called the "stemless lady's slipper" because its two broad leaves spring from the ground at the base of the flower stalk. In the other lady's slippers the leaves climb the stem. Please don't pick these lovely flowers for a corsage. They don't last the way hothouse orchids do, but soon go limp. If you must have them for your own, make a collection of kodachromes instead. Such a project will take you into the most beautiful places this side of heaven—cool glades, fern beds, mossy bogs, secluded ravines. The most wonderful thing about orchids is the setting in which they grow.

Beside the lady's slippers there are several exotic-looking rose-pink orchids such as the arethusa shown on page 69. Then there are fringed varieties which grow in densely flowered spikes— purple-fringed, yellow-fringed, white-fringed, and green-fringed orchids. In a class by itself is the showy orchis (lower right) which comes into bloom at

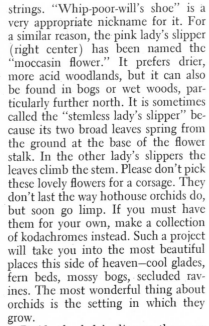

Pink Lady's Slipper

Showy Orchis

49

Wild Pink

Mountain Laurel

Tulip-tree Flower

Dogwood

the time the warblers are migrating through. If you look sharply you might find its two-colored flowers, white and lavender, shyly returning your glance from a leafy spot in the forest.

When spring has come to stay there is a great display of flowers for a spell, then a lull, before the long procession of summer bloom gets under way. The wild pink (upper left) is one of the gayer members of this spring show. From New England to the mountains of the Carolinas it covers rocky slopes and sandy, gravelly places with its tussocks of pink blossoms.

Feel the stem of a wild pink. You will find it sticky. This is not to discourage you from picking it but to trap ants and other unwanted insects which are too small to be useful in pollination. When an ant crawls up the stalk it finds its feet caught in a mess of glue. In that way is the supply of nectar protected, saved for the bees or for other insects large enough to do some good. The mountain laurel has a similar device. Its flowers are mounted on hairy stems which ooze a sticky substance.

The mountain laurel, which covers whole hillsides in the Appalachians with a riot of bloom in June, is just one of the many shrubs and trees which possess spectacular flowers. Some of them are shown on these two pages. Sunday tourists who break off branches and fill the back seat of the car with them are vandals, nothing less, for these woody plants take much longer to grow than do other flowers.

The tulip-tree's blossoms escape our notice when held aloft, as they often are, eighty or a hundred feet in the air, but when they are borne on a branch which droops low enough we might examine the fantastic yellow-green cups. Bees, attracted by the tawny orange centers, push their broad shoulders against the strategically placed stamens and pistils. A relative of the magnolias, the tulip-tree (shown in its entirety on page 44) is unlike any other American tree. Certainly its blossoms are like those of no other.

The dogwood (lower left) is also rather unique although there is a similar species in the West which has six "petals" instead of four. Actually what we call petals are not petals at all. They are modified white leaves, known as *bracts*. The real blossoms, tiny yellow-green flowers, nestle in the center of these showy white bracts. In late April and early May the white masses of the flowering dogwood and the bright rose-pink of the redbud decorate the forest margins and understory as if in celebration of the arrival of the warblers. It is a festive time of a year—a wonderful time of year to be alive.

The purest pink in all the wood is probably that of the pink azalea or wild honeysuckle. This shrub, a mass of breath-taking bloom, stands four or five feet tall, sometimes six, living proof that beauty is its own excuse for being. Some states recognize this and give the azalea full protection of the law. Both it and the rhododendron or great laurel like sour soils, in rocky woodlands or in swamps. Old rhododendrons might reach a height of forty feet, forming impenetrable thickets from which black-throated blue and Canada warblers may sing (if in the mountains) or hooded warblers if in a bog. There are many species of rhododendrons in various parts of the world. One, the exquisite Lapland rhododendron, only a few inches high, grows above timberline on Mount Washington and on Katahdin.

Pink Azalea

Rhododendron

51

Mourning Cloak Butterfly and Butterfly Weed

BUTTERFLIES AND MOTHS OF WOODLAND EDGES

Beauty, a distinguished naturalist contends, "is not a slave to purpose. . . . It is sheer delightful waste, to be enjoyed in its own high right." The beauty of a butterfly's wings bears this out. Whereas we may be repulsed by a crawling roach we react very differently to a butterfly. Yet both are insects.

No one knows exactly how many butterflies and moths there are. At least 120,000 species have been named in the world and new ones are constantly being described. Of these the moths are by far the most numerous. Some are so tiny as to merit the term *microlepidoptera*. On the other hand, the largest ones such as the giant silkworms, some of which are shown on the page opposite, average larger than our largest butterflies.

Butterflies, on the whole, are a gayer lot, very important to the natural economy. They, the bees, flower flies, and some of the moths and beetles pollinate the flowers and keep the green world green. Were it not for them, much life would perish.

In no one locality would you find as many species of butterflies as you would birds, but the total for eastern North America is about the same. Some are very local. For example, only where turtlehead grows will you find colonies of the Baltimore checkerspot.

Whereas the Baltimore checkerspot, an attractive little black and orange butterfly, may live only a month, the mourning cloak (upper left) may live at least six or eight months, perhaps nearly a full year. It is one of the small group of butterflies which hibernate,

Red-spotted Purple Butterfly and Orange Hawkweed

tucking themselves away in hollow trees, or in dark corners. Occasionally they sally forth during a warm January thaw, only to be chilled by a sudden freeze. In England where it is known as the Camberwell beauty, this species which comes overseas from Scandinavia is the great prize of British collectors.

The red-spotted purple is another butterfly which prefers the wood roads and woodland edges even though it is shown here on an orange hawkweed, a field plant.

The ghostly luna ("moon moth") dances like a gossamer-winged fairy about street lights on summer nights. No other moth can equal it in beauty. Pale pea-green with a furry white body and streaming tails, it is sometimes found clinging to the trunk of a tree after it has emerged from its cocoon among the fallen leaves. Like all adults of the giant silkworm group, it lives but a few days for it cannot eat. Its mouthparts are tiny and useless.

The cecropia is our largest moth (6-6½ inches). Its spindle-shaped cocoons, fastened lengthwise on the twigs are a familiar sight on shade trees even in cities like New York. Should you find one, shake it. If it gives forth a light dry rattle it is probably parasitized by ichneumon wasps. A solid thump means it is good. Take it home and hatch it out.

Nearly as large as the cecropia is the polyphemus, tan with great owl-like "eyes." Its oval cocoon dangles from a flimsy silken cord, often drops.

The regal moth belongs to a different family. Its larva, covered with long curved spines is the most fearsome-looking of all caterpillars. Country people call it "hickory horn devil."

Luna Moth

Cecropia Moth

Polyphemus Moth

Regal Moth

Box Turtle

Red Newt

REPTILES AND AMPHIBIANS OF THE WOODLANDS

When a turtle lives on land we often call it a tortoise. Whether we call the armor-plated reptile at the left a box turtle or a box tortoise makes little difference. Gayly marked with splashes of yellow or orange, it ambles through the dewy grass and shuffles among the dead leaves looking for succulent green shoots. A vegetarian would contend that here is living proof of the secret of longevity, for a box turtle might live a century. All turtles are protected by a rounded carapace above and flat plastron beneath. When worried they pull in head, tail, and feet, but the box turtle goes its relatives one better. It has a hinge on its plastron which enables it to close so tightly that a knife blade can scarcely slip inside the shell.

Crawling over the forest floor on damp days are red newts, or more properly speaking, red efts, the land stage of the newt. A newt lives the first part of its life in the water as a dingy greenish little animal, but turns orange when it abandons its pond. Later, when it returns to the water to lay its eggs and finish out its life, it again becomes greenish. Some people think newts are lizards, but they are not. They are *salamanders*, amphibians related to the frogs and toads. Salamanders are usually moist, whereas lizards are dry and scaly like snakes and other reptiles. The blue-tailed skink, shown opposite, is a lizard. The one with the blue tail is a young one, the redhead is an old male. Often called the "five-lined skink," it is the only lizard known to occur as far north as New England.

On the other hand, there are many salamanders in the North. In brief, salamanders prefer things damp and cool (in spite of the legend that they can stand great heat). Lizards like it dry and hot.

In the same woods where the red eft lives we may find the wood frog, tan with a black mask across its eyes. The little gray tree frog is seen less often, but its short purring trill is a familiar sound in early summer.

One can spend his entire life roaming the woods yet never see a poisonous snake such as a copperhead or rattlesnake. Copperheads can still be found in the Palisades on the outskirts of New York City. A few survive in the Blue Hills near Boston, and it is even possible to find one within the limits of Washington, D.C., probably carried down the Potomac on the flood waters. But so retiring are copperheads that you might never see one unless you search out the rocky dens where they hibernate. They have the faculty of following the invisible trails of other snakes which have passed by earlier. In this way they eventually congregate in some deep ledge, often in the company of rattlers and black snakes.

One is as likely to be killed by lightning as by a venomous snake. Most snakes, of course, are harmless. In fact many are good mousers. If your reaction when you see one is to run away screaming or to pick up a club and beat it to death you never will learn much about them. Do not believe all the "un-natural" history that is circulated about these lowly creatures. A horsehair kept in water will not turn into a snake; milk snakes do not milk cows; nor do young snakes escape into their parents open mouths.

Treetoad

Wood Frog

Blue-tailed Skink

Copperhead

Raccoon

Gray Fox

New York Weasel

MAMMALS OF
THE WOODLANDS

When the last wood thrush goes to bed, the four-footed things venture forth. Because most mammals are nocturnal we don't know as much about them as we do about birds. The childlike tracks of raccoons may be found by the riverbank, but how many men have ever seen the animal itself unless he has treed it with a pack of "coon dawgs" on a moonlit night? Yet almost every large woodland has its raccoon family, providing there is a hollow tree large enough for a den, and particularly if there is water. For raccoons are very fastidious. They wash not only their roots and berries, but even their frogs and crawfish.

After dark the rabbits at the edges of the fields must watch out for the gray fox which might at any moment leap from the shadows. Although not as northern as the red fox (page 31), it is found throughout a large part of the United States.

Whereas a gray fox may have an area of one or two square miles for its hunting preserve, a weasel patrols about 100 acres. Sinuous and streamlined, weasels efficiently track down their prey, mostly mice, but also any animals they can overcome, even rabbits. The night is full of violence for the small rodents. Weasels in the North trade their brown coats for white ones when winter comes, becoming the "ermine" of commerce.

The opossum, that nocturnal prowler which sometimes ambles across the road in front of the car, has been spreading lately, until it is now quite common as far north as New York State and Michigan. It is a *Marsupial*, one of those mammals which carries its babies in a pouch the way a kangaroo does. For several weeks the young, so small that a dozen would scarcely fill a tablespoon, remain in the pouch; later they may ride on their mother's back, wrapping their ratlike tails about hers. When a possum is chased it heads for the nearest tree, but if it can't reach one it might just play dead, hence the term "playing possum."

Opossum

Although most squirrels go about their business during the daytime, the flying squirrel is an exception. It comes forth at dusk, gliding from tree to tree, using the broad flaps between the front and hind legs as sails. Should you pound on a hollow tree where flying squirrels spend the day, one after another will pop forth and stare wonderingly with big dreamy eyes.

In our rambles through the woods we sometimes surprise a deer which bounds away, flashing its white "flag," but dusk is the best time to see them. Then they come into the open, munching a twig here, and a few tender shoots somewhere else. Recent inventories show that the white-tailed deer now numbers over five million in the U.S. Today they can be seen at the very outskirts of big cities like New York where they had been unknown for nearly a century. Wise regulations, allowing the herds to increase while still affording sport, have made this dramatic comeback possible. Wisconsin leads with a deer population of nine hundred thousand. In fact, in places the population is so high that some starve to death in winter. No animal can ever exceed its food supply. Healthy woods and waters mean more food for more wild life.

Flying Squirrel

White-tailed Deer

57

Pileated Woodpecker

Ruffed Grouse

Wood Thrush

BIRDS OF THE WOODLANDS

Thirty or forty years ago ornithologists thought that the big crow-sized pileated woodpecker was going to follow the ivory-bill to extinction. In some states, such as New Jersey, it disappeared entirely. Then something happened: the birds that remained seemed to become more adaptable. They did not withdraw into the last primeval forests, but tried to make the best of things in second-growth woodland. This new strain has repopulated county after county, state after state, until this wonderful bird can now be found as close to New York City as the Palisades and at the very outskirts of Washington, D. C. The "log cock," as it is sometimes called, is here to stay. It is regrettable that the ivory-bill (page 15) was unable to make a similar compromise with civilization.

A woodlot is always better for woodpeckers, and for the hole-nesting birds that depend on the woodpeckers, when the trees are eighty or a hundred years old. But the little downy woodpecker (lower right) seems to get by almost anywhere; in a neglected orchard, among the shade trees, or even in a vacant brush lot where it hammers open the tough cocoons of saturnid moths or the dry galls on the stems of goldenrods. Woodpeckers never eat wood as some people think but are, in a manner of speaking, tree surgeons which dig out the borers and carpenter ants.

Although pheasants and quail far exceed it in the amount of sport they furnish, the ruffed grouse is voted by many sportsmen the finest of all game birds. It might be rusty red or quite gray;

there are two distinct color phases, with much variation in between, but it can always be identified, when it flushes with a great whir, by its broad fanlike tail with a black band near the tip. Grouse are woodland birds, subject to puzzling fluctuations, reaching a peak of abundance, then crashing to a population so low that sportsmen fear their extinction. Some have thought this to be cyclic, pointing out that the crash seems to come every ten or eleven years, but further study has shown that it is not as regular as that.

Grouse thrive best in woods which have a mixture of hardwoods and evergreens, where there are small clearings, wood roads, and adjacent fields to let in a little sun. But if cattle are allowed to graze in the woodlot, the undergrowth so important to grouse is destroyed. Frank Edminster in his classic book on the ruffed grouse concludes that forest management is the secret to more grouse and that killing of predators not only doesn't pay, it doesn't even work. For though some predators take grouse, their rôle in maintaining the rodent balance is even more important to grouse welfare.

Among winged predators the red-tailed hawk, which slowly wheels high in the blue, is one of the most valuable rodent destroyers. It roams the sky over every state in the Union. The barred owl which belongs to the night shift is primarily eastern, living in river swamps and bottomland woods. It has an eight-hoot call, *hoohoo-hoohoo - - - - - - hoohoo-hoohoo*, more baritone than the bass hoots of the horned owl. The latter bird prefers the drier woodlands and hills.

Most breathtaking of all songbirds that brighten eastern woodlands is the

Red-tailed Hawk

Barred Owl

Downy Woodpecker

Scarlet Tanager

Chickadee

Rose-breasted Grosbeak

scarlet tanager. It is unbelievably red. Out of a family of four hundred tanagers garbed in every hue of the rainbow, the scarlet tanager is the only one pioneering enough to fly to eastern Canada each year. It comes by night, taking advantage of the southerly winds which act as an express highway for migrants from the tropics. In the morning we find it, sitting quietly in the oaks, seemingly tired, and well it might be, for it has probably covered three or four thousand miles during the previous fortnight or two.

Whereas the song of the tanager is burry, like a robin with a sore throat, the rose-breasted grosbeak (below) sounds like a robin who has taken voice lessons from a master. Its mellow notes are given with great feeling. Tanagers haunt the bigger trees, while the rose-breast prefers second growth where redstarts sing, saplings twenty or thirty years old, or thickets of elderberries and willows along the riverbank. The male is one of the most striking of all American birds; its mate is streaked, suggesting an overgrown sparrow.

Tanagers, grosbeaks, and the warblers (opposite) are brief tenants of the woodlands during the summer, but the chickadee (left center) and its companions the nuthatches, titmice, and woodpeckers hold the fort throughout the year, examining every stub and twig for sleeping insects which the summer crowd has missed. They are grateful for a handout, however, so if you would have them about your home put out suet for them.

Warblers are often called the butterflies of the bird world. Fifty-four species are known north of the Mexican boundary and their total number of individuals certainly exceeds a billion.

Hooded Warbler

Redstart

Cerulean Warbler

Black-throated Blue Warbler

Two billion is probably a shrewder guess. Bird-watching would lose half its glamour were it not for this colorful horde, at least in the East. It is possible to see twenty-five species or more in a day during a good "wave" in May. The greater number pass through to the North Woods country, but even in the deciduous forest, one bird in six, during the summer months, is a warbler of some kind.

The hooded warbler, golden with a black hood surrounding its yellow face, is found all through the South, both in the wooded swamps and in the Appalachian hills as far north as New York State and the Great Lakes. Its bright song is characteristic of rhododendron and laurel thickets.

The redstart, widespread in much of the continent, is one of the most abundant birds in the Appalachian belt, in some places second in number only to the red-eyed vireo. Nesting from the mountains of Georgia all the way to Newfoundland, its numbers must be in the high millions. Its preference is for small trees—birches, aspens, and other saplings twenty or thirty feet high.

The cerulean warbler, at home in the forests of the Mississippi Valley, is unknown along the coast. It usually forages so high in the trees that its blue back cannot be seen, but the narrow dark ring across its white breast is always a good field mark. Another bluish-backed species, the black-throated blue warbler, nests throughout the higher Appalachian hills as well as in the mixed forests of the Canadian border. Like the hooded warbler, it frequents the understory, the thickets of azalea, laurel, and rhododendron.

Towhee

Brown Thrasher

BIRDS OF THE PINE BARRENS

Great pine barrens extend down the coastal plain from Cape Cod to Florida. Even though the scraggly pines which form them have needles and cones, we don't think of them in the same way that we do of the cool forests of hemlock and fir further north. Nor can they be classed with the deciduous forests. They are woodlands of a different sort. The famous New Jersey pine barrens which cover many hundreds of square miles are almost uninhabited, so sandy and sterile is the soil, yet they are only an hour's drive from populous Philadelphia. New-Yorkers, in a two hours' drive out on Long Island, see similar barrens.

The nature of the pine barrens changes as one goes southward along the coast. On Cape Cod, Long Island, and in New Jersey the pitch pine is the dominant tree. But so repeatedly are these barrens burned that nowadays these short-needled pines seldom get more than twenty or thirty feet high. Knee-deep scrub oak covers much of the monotonous landscape. In coastal Maryland and Virginia, where the soil is apparently richer, the loblolly becomes the most noticeable pine. Un-like the squat pitch pine it grows tall and clean, forming flat-topped groves between whose trunks the sky is plainly visible. When we reach coastal Carolina the long-leaf pine, with needles more than a foot long, appears and from there to Florida it becomes the most familiar tree in the "piney woods."

Pine barrens seldom have the variety of birds that most other woodlands support. However, we are sure to find some of the same birds which live in other brushy places, familiar birds like field sparrows, catbirds, towhees, and brown thrashers. But these are by no means confined to the barrens. Neither are the flickers (lower right), and downy and hairy woodpeckers, which forage on the fire-killed stubs. To most woodpeckers a dead tree is a dead tree, no matter whether it is in the pine barrens, in a river swamp or a mountain forest. But not so to the red-cockaded woodpecker (right center). It must have pines. Old-timers say this zebra-backed species is not seen nearly as often as it was in their youth, but if you search diligently you might still find it in certain groves from the Caro-

62

linas to Florida. Its white cheeks are its best field mark.

There are usually chickadees, yellow-throats, blue jays, and crows in most pine barrens. An occasional red-tailed hawk might be seen soaring in circles and if the country is wild enough, the stentorian hoots of the great horned owl may be heard after dark.

In the Northeast there are two birds which we look for specifically when we drive through the barrens—the pine warbler, which trills like a musical chipping sparrow from the taller trees, and the prairie warbler (upper right) which sings its wiry ascending notes from the oak scrub. One observer remarked that the prairie warbler's song sounded to him "like a mouse with a tooth ache." Although the pine warbler is well named, the prairie warbler is not, for it neither warbles nor lives in prairies.

Once we have stopped to tick these two birds off on our check-lists we usually head directly for the coast, where on the beaches, marshes, and inlets we shall surely find a great many more exciting birds than we shall in the barrens.

However, as one goes further south the "piney woods" become more interesting. Not only is there a chance of the red-cockaded woodpecker, but also of the yellow-throated warbler, brown-headed nuthatch, and pinewoods sparrow. The latter bird, a plain little creature, is one of the finest singers in all the South, a sparrow that plays on the thrush's instrument.

Pine barrens are of greater interest to the botanist than to the bird watcher, because in the sandy places, in the sour soil, and in the bogs grow rare gentians, orchids, and other unique flowers found nowhere else.

Prairie Warbler

Red-cockaded Woodpecker

Flicker

63

THE NORTH WOODS COUNTRY
The Coniferous Forest

Spreading across the northern edge of the United States from Maine to Minnesota are the North Woods, vacationland to millions of Americans. Extending north to Hudson Bay, and from Newfoundland across the broad expanse of Canada to Alaska, the great coniferous forest covers at least two million square miles. Ever since the last ice age it has been slowly extending its vast dominion toward the pole. Tamaracks and willows are the pioneers. They are the last stunted trees one sees as one goes northward. From this point—tree limit—to the Arctic Sea it is all tundra, frozen soil which thaws briefly each summer for only a few inches at the surface, but not deeply enough to nourish trees.

Whereas deciduous trees drop their leaves when winter comes, and become quite naked, the aspect of the conifers remains unchanged, except for the snow that often lies deep upon them. Only one, the tamarack, drops its needles. The long thrust of Arctic air which drives down every winter from the pole makes melancholy music in the evergreen boughs, whispering, sighing, moaning. Most mammals are then taking the long sleep, and few birds are to be found. The warblers and many of the others are deep in the tropics; only the stout-hearted chickadees, roving bands of crossbills, and a few others remain.

In the mountains, if one climbs high enough, he may find stands of cool coniferous forest as far south as the high Smokies in North Carolina. Altitude compensates for latitude, and in these islands of spruce and balsam live many of the same birds and mammals that we speak of as "Canadian" species.

The North Woods is the land of

64

Christmas trees, millions of dark spires pointing to the sky. Twenty-one million Christmas trees are harvested each year in the United States alone, and millions more in Canada. Most of these are spruce and balsam. Some moralists deplore this annual sacrifice of millions of young trees for momentary pleasure, but as Donald Culross Peattie points out in his fascinating book, A Natural History of Trees, the proper selection of little trees will merely result in the betterment of the stand. He writes: ". . . out of every ten young trees in the forest nine are destined to lose out and die. No harm, but only good, can follow from the proper cutting of young Christmas trees. And the destiny of Balsam, loveliest of them all, would otherwise too often be excelsior, or boards for packing cases, or newsprint bringing horror on its face into your home. Far better that the little tree should arrive, like a shining child at your door, breathing of all out of doors and cupping healthy North Woods cold between its boughs, to bring delight to human children."

Spring comes slowly to the North Country. It gets underway when the ice, thundering like distant cannon, goes out of the lakes. It is then that the long wavering wedges of geese arrive, to tarry awhile before continuing on to their lonely nesting grounds on the tundra. By April the robins are back even though the snow still lies deep on the cool slopes. Even in May many nights are cold enough to leave a skin of ice on the ponds, and once in a while a late snow flurry turns back the calendar. May is an uncertain month, but when the dam finally breaks a great flood of bird migrants pours in. Each day sees new arrivals. Some have not been present for more than eight months, for their sojourn in the North Country is brief. They make the long trip solely to have elbow room in which to raise their families, and to exploit the abundant insect food supply which is available during the short northern summer. Some, like the blackpoll warbler or the gray-cheeked thrush which nest near tree-limit, make a round trip of ten thousand miles or more. In spite of the hazardous journey there is great survival value in this. A bird with four or five mouths to feed needs a plot of ground that is large enough to support its family. Canada offers a summer homestead to many hundreds of millions of migrants. Think of the competition there would be in the tropics if they all remained there during this trying period!

Men make their annual pilgrimage to the North Woods for other reasons; to leave tension behind, to relax, and to enjoy cool days while the cities swelter. A man may swim in the bracing water of any of the tens of thousands of lakes which dot the spruce country, he may play the pioneer, portaging with his canoe from one hidden lake to another, or he may fish. These boreal waters are seldom defiled by the sewage of cities or the silt of eroded farms, so fishing is usually good unless a pulp mill has contributed its sour poisons. From Maine to Minnesota summer camps by the hundreds give boys and girls their first taste of woodcraft and nature study. It is plain, then, that as a summer playground the North Woods has a value as great as the newsprint it furnishes, perhaps greater, for it gives us new vitality and spirit, whereas the bad news which shrieks from every headline is corrosive.

65

White Birch

Tamarack

TREES OF
THE NORTH WOODS

Birches and aspens are not conifers, but they are part and parcel of the North Woods, a stage in succession. When the pines and spruces are cut down, birches and aspens often replace them. The white birch, once used by Indians for their birch-bark canoes, has chalky white bark which can be peeled off in horizontal bands. But pray do not peel it from a living tree, for ugly black rings will mark it forever after. The yellow birch, the largest of the family, has bark that is dull golden with many shaggy ends hanging free.

The tamarack is a contradiction in terms, a deciduous evergreen. Its inch-long needles, arranged in tufts along the twigs, drop to the ground in the fall. Except for dwarf willows it is the tree which goes farthest north.

The hemlock, with its short flat needles, is a slow-growing tree. Nurtured in the shade of other forest trees it finally takes over to form dark shady stands of its own. It likes cool ravines where trout streams cascade over the rocks.

Many people know the balsam only as a Christmas tree, to be desired because of its fine symmetry and because its needles are less prickly than those of a spruce. But to others its spire is the most perfect symbol of the Canadian wilderness.

White pine, the tree that founded a lumber empire, can be told from other pines by its needles which come five in a cluster. Graceful and dignified, it has played a greater rôle in American history than any other tree.

Hemlock

Balsam Fir

Yellow Birch

White Pine

Indian Pipe

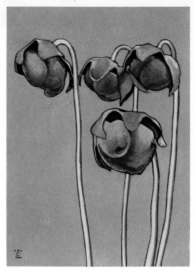

Pitcher-plant

PLANTS OF THE NORTH WOODS COUNTRY

Somehow the plants that hide in the bogs and among the moss and ferns of the cool coniferous country have a sort of glamour unmatched by the coarser and more familiar flowers of the roadside. Perhaps glamour is not the word, for theirs is a subtle beauty, such as our native orchids possess.

The Indian pipe, ghostly and colorless, springs from the pine needles and leaf mold in shady places. It might be called a parasite, because it derives its sustenance from decaying wood. Therefore it does not need green tissue, as other plants do, in the manufacture of its food.

The pitcher-plant, which lives in oozy sphagnum bogs, is said to be carnivorous. Its leaves (not shown in the picture above) are shaped like slender purplish pitchers, and are usually half-full of water. The lip of the pitcher is covered with stiff downward-pointing hairs, which make it impossible for any insect trapped in the jug to get out. Whether this curious plant actually digests its drowned prey we don't know. Biologists point out that the larvæ of mosquitoes are sometimes hatched and reared in the stagnant liquid.

Arethusa, one of the most breathtaking of the smaller orchids, has been so sought after that it has disappeared from one bog after another. It is rapidly becoming extinct within the limits of the United States. You must go further north into Canada to be sure of finding it. In the cold red sphagnum bogs of Newfoundland it is perhaps as abundant as it ever was and even from the windows of the little narrow-gauge railway which traverses that foggy island you can sometimes see patches of pink formed by hundreds of these exquisite orchids.

The twinflower or linnæa was Linnæus' favorite flower, and to it he gave his own name (Linnæa borealis). At Hammerby, his country home in Sweden, one can see his tea service decorated with a border of these dangling pink bells. A portrait of this great taxonomist who devised the system of scientific names which we all use shows him holding one of the delicate plants in his hand. The twinflower, growing throughout the boreal forests of the world, is equally at home in Sweden, New England, or our Northwest.

Of the dozen species of trilliums listed in Gray's Manual, the painted trillium is the most beautiful, a favorite of wildflower gardeners. In late spring, about the time the warblers are back on territory this three-parted flower with its bloodshot petals is a familiar sight in the acid woodlands of upstate New York and New England.

Like the twinflower and certain other northern plants, many mushrooms are found in both the Old World and the New. In spite of its reputation of being deadly, the beautiful fly amanita, shown here, probably never causes the death of a healthy person. Eating it results in hallucinations and delirium, perhaps severe stomach cramps, but following a period of stupor the victim usually recovers. In ancient Scandinavia, the Norsemen ate it to go berserk; certain Siberian tribes use it to excite excessive emotion; Rumanians put it on the windowsill to kill flies, and in our own country Walt Disney used it in his fantastic ballet of the mushrooms in *Fantasia*.

Arethusa

Twinflower

Painted Trillium

Fly Amanita

Moose

Black Bear

Snowshoe Rabbit

MAMMALS OF
THE NORTH WOODS

In parts of Maine, large cloven hoof-prints, more pointed than the prints of a cow, can be found in the peaty earth. These are the tracks of the moose, the biggest beast in the North Woods. Larger than a horse, it might stand seven feet at the withers and weigh fifteen hundred pounds. Its rounded nose, great palmate antlers, and the hump on its shoulders make it a most impressive anmial, a goliath compared to the delicately formed deer with which it shares the wilderness. The best place to look for a moose is in a sheltered cove of some secluded lake where waterlilies grow. There, if lucky, you may see the big animal, with water up to its middle, pulling up the aquatic plants by the roots. Although deer have prospered in late years, there are but a fraction of the moose that once waded the edges of northern lakes. South of the Canadian border they are completely gone from a number of states where they once were known.

Although the black bear is found to the limit of trees in Canada it is by no means confined to the North Woods. In fact, it is the only big game animal originally found in all forty-eight states. It still lives in thirty-five of them and its U.S. population is estimated to be over 130,000. The big, inquisitive, flat-footed carnivore has been slowly increasing again in recent years.

The snowshoe rabbit is the rabbit of the coniferous country. Some prefer

70

to call it the varying hare because it changes its brown summer pelage when winter comes, becoming pure white except for the black tips of its ears. The snowshoe rabbit goes through a cycle every ten years or so, becoming abundant, then crashing.

The red squirrel, or chickaree, scolds the stranger wherever he sets foot in the evergreen forest. Although spruce cones, birch seeds, and mushrooms make up much of the diet of this jittery little acrobat, it eats all the birds' eggs it can get its little paws on during the month of June. Luckily, the big horned owls enjoy eating red squirrels, so things tend to balance fairly well in the spruce forest's economy.

The pine marten, a large weasel, can outrun a squirrel in the treetops. It once ranged widely throughout the dense evergreen forests, but has retreated before the advance of civilization until now it is one of the rarest of the fur-bearers. Its inquisitive nature makes it easy to trap.

There are many legends about the wolverine, a powerfully built member of the weasel family. Trappers say it follows their trap lines, slyly eating the bait without being caught. They insist it is so surly that even a bear will turn aside if the two meet on the trail. Like the marten, the wolverine has been pushed northward toward Hudson Bay by civilization.

The porcupine will always survive. No one wants its prickly hide, and all that it demands of life is a bellyful of bark once in a while from an evergreen tree. Usually the trees need thinning anyway. Porcupines do not shoot their quills, but if a dog gets too close a sudden slap of the tail will leave a fistful of quills in its nose.

Red Squirrel

Pine Marten

Wolverine

Porcupine

71

Red Crossbill

Ruby-crowned Kinglet

Blackburnian Warbler

Bay-breasted Warbler

BIRDS OF
THE NORTH WOODS

A few birds stay in the North Woods throughout the cold months. Such a one is the red crossbill (left) with its curious snipper bill with which it opens spruce cones. Crossbills may wander in a lemming-like way when the cones give out, or for some other more obscure reason, but winter's cold does not seem to bother them.

The tiny kinglets are not so hardy. Although some golden-crowns might stay north of the Canadian boundary, most of them migrate to the southern states along with the ruby-crowned kinglets. They both return before the warblers arrive.

Sample censuses in Maine and Canada indicate that the number of birds in a good spruce forest during June might average five or six per acre. Well over half would be warblers. Multiplying this by the immense acreage of wooded Canada, think of the astronomical numbers of warblers there must be! Nashville warblers and yellow-throats live in the bogs, magnolia and myrtle warblers flit in and out of the young balsams, black-throated green warblers sing from the lower branches of the bigger trees while the Blackburnian warbler (left), its throat ablaze, sings its wiry song from the higher branches. Each kind has its niche.

During a spruce budworm outbreak in Canada, ninety-two pairs of bay-breasted warblers (lower left) were recorded on a hundred acres—all raising families too. Inasmuch as a warbler might feed its young every four or five minutes it would be hard to believe that they do not make great inroads on the insect pests.

The male purple finch looks like a sparrow which has been dipped in raspberry juice. It nests at the edges of open park-like spots in the spruce forest, but we are more likely to see it during migration or in winter. Like some of the other northern finches, it is a great wanderer, here in numbers one year, almost absent the next. We are delighted when the nomadic flocks visit our feeding trays.

Purple Finch

The red-breasted nuthatch, another erratic visitor, may come southward with the flood of warblers in September, or it may stay north so that we scarcely see one all winter. Just why, we don't know. Some say it is because of the food supply, but this has never been proved. To find the red-breast we listen for a note that is higher and more nasal than that of the familiar white-breasted nuthatch, like a "baby" nuthatch or a tiny tin horn.

Red-breasted Nuthatch

The sapsucker is our most migratory woodpecker. Some travel from Canada to the West Indies or Mexico. Rows of neat holes in the trunks of trees indicate its presence. After drilling the holes the bird makes the rounds, sopping up the oozing sap with its bristly tongue. With such food habits you can see why it must leave the North Country where everything freezes in winter.

Yellow-bellied Sapsucker

The spruce grouse is often called the "fool hen" because it is so trusting or "witless"—call it what you will—that it will often allow a man to knock it over with a stick. For this reason it has never been as satisfactory a game bird as the ruffed grouse. It has all but disappeared from great tracts of spruce forest where it once lived.

Spruce Grouse

WATER, LIFE BLOOD OF THE EARTH
The Streams, Rivers, and Lakes

Each year, fifteen hundred cubic miles of water fall on the United States, enough, if it fell in one simultaneous cloudburst, to cover the country to a depth of two and one-half feet. Two million miles of streams, forming a vast network of capillaries, veins, and arteries, carry this precious life blood to every part of the land and finally to the sea.

Soil without water will not support life. To test this, try the following experiment. Spade up two chunks of earth, about a foot square, and put each in a pail. Sprinkle one with water every day, keep the other dry. Soon shoots of green will appear in the well-watered bucket, blades of grass and small weeds. Meanwhile in the other

pail the earth will dry out, crack, and whatever life there was will die.

It is logical, then, that the best places for wildlife are close to water. That is why bird watchers always head for the nearest pond or swamp. That is why botanists often find the low country more rewarding than the drier uplands. Mammals, insects, amphibians, and reptiles—all are more numerous around wet places.

When a raindrop falls and starts its long pilgrimage to the sea its journey should be a slow one, not a race. At most it should be an obstacle race. First the crystal drop should be checked in its precipitous plunge by the broad leaves of trees or by the thick matting of grass, then allowed to drip to the soil where, clear and clean, it sinks slowly through the humus. It may be sucked up immediately by a thirsty root or it might find its way to an underground spring. The spring might bubble forth to join a brook—a clear brook, if the banks are held in place by a healthy growth of plants. Should the stream be blocked by a beaver dam, the water backs up until it finally finds its way through the chinks and crevices. As it meanders onward the stream grows larger, loitering in coves and marshy pockets, and swings placidly in broad oxbows through the farming country.

The chances are probably three to one that our raindrop will never reach the sea, that it will be used up somewhere along the way. That is as it should be. The slower the journey the better chance to do some good.

The first settlers found ·crystal streams teeming with fish, luxuriant forests, and waving seas of grass. Wildlife was everywhere. But today many rivers, once clean enough to drink, run thick with mud. Streams that were anglers' paradises no longer are fit for fish to live in.

How different is the journey of many a raindrop in this, the twentieth century! It falls with a splash, unchecked by leaves or grass. It finds no litter of humus to hold it until it can sink into the parched earth. Joined by an army of other raindrops it wets the surface of the ground, seals it, and trickles into the nearest rivulet. Rushing headlong, the uncontrolled water cuts away the banks, which add their brown mud to the torrent. Where the beaver dam used to be there is nothing to slow the rushing water. The beavers were trapped off long ago. The swamps which once acted as pockets for the high water to back into have been ditched and drained. So by the time our muddy creek reaches the big river there is a great flood. High water from a hundred brooks and tributaries have reached the same place at the same time. Houses are swept away and lives are lost.

Too much water in early spring often means too little in the summer. The water has rushed off the land too fast, and when the hot days of August come, all but a few pools are dry.

The mud that chokes our rivers and harbors costs our country hundreds of millions of dollars each year: millions in hard cash for dredging alone, and millions more for the damage to fish and wildlife. When the water is choked with silt, water plants do not get enough sunlight. They die, fish die, and waterfowl disappear.

This is all the result of erosion, the wearing away of the land, caused when some lumber company upstream has denuded the headwaters or has scalped the hilltops; when a careless camper has burned a thousand acres and destroyed the humus; when some farmer found it easier to plow his furrows up and down hill rather across the slopes where they would hold the rainwater.

In many streams pollution is the killer. A little organic pollution does no harm, but too much destroys oxygen and shuts out the sunlight in the same way that silt does. Chemical waste dumped by factories is even more toxic.

Erosion and pollution are like poisons coursing through the blood of a sick continent. The National Wildlife Federation, the Izaac Walton League, and other conservation organizations are fighting to return the patient to health.

Black Willow   Weeping Willow

TREES OF THE STREAMSIDE

Trees are the guardians of our streams. No farm should ever be plowed to the river's edge. For a few furrows gained by removing the willows, the beauty of a streamside is lost, and wildlife is robbed of a home and a highway. The banks, no longer held together by roots, are cut away by freshets, and the fields add their good earth to the torrent.

Of the many willows in America, twenty-four can be classified as trees. All are more useful as anchors of the soil than they are for charcoal, crates, or any of the other uses to which they are sometimes put. Of all this scrubby thin-leaved tribe, the black willow is the largest, occasionally reaching 120 feet. The weeping willow, a native of China, was first planted in cemeteries,

because its drooping foliage suggested sorrow, but many now grow wild along our streams.

The cottonwood, the largest of the poplar tribe, is the fastest-growing tree. It has been known to attain 100 feet in fifteen years. The sycamore, identified by its patchy white trunk, is the most massive eastern tree. It is a favorite den tree of many mammals. The box elder, a maple with leaves suggesting those of an ash, attracts evening grosbeaks when these big yellow finches visit the East on their winter wanderings. They eagerly eat the winged "keys." The silver maple, with deep-cut leaves, silvery beneath, is often planted in towns as are most of the other attractive river trees shown on this page and the page opposite.

76

Cottonwood

Sycamore

Box Elder

Silver Maple

Beaver

Otter

MAMMALS OF THE STREAMS

The beaver's fur, once used in making ugly stovepipe hats, was what really sparked the conquest of the West. Trappers were ahead of all the famous explorers. They preceded Lewis and Clark. Cities were founded and minor wars were fought, all because of beavers. It is no wonder that their millions melted away, first from the East, then from the Midwest, and finally from one watershed after another in the far West. Its fur is valuable enough, but only in recent years have we been able to estimate the beaver's true value. As an upstream engineer each one is worth many times the price its pelt will bring. Our government knows this and has been releasing beavers in the headwaters of many western streams. There these industrious paddle-tailed animals build dams free, dams which would otherwise cost several thousand dollars each to construct. These dams slow up the streams where it does the most good, thereby controlling floods. At the same time future meadows are being created. You see, a beaver dam, like any other dam, catches all the mud that is carried downstream, and eventually chokes up. The beavers then go elsewhere—upstream or down—to build a new dam. When the old dam goes to pieces and the pond water recedes, the bed of black silt becomes a meadow. Today, thousands of acres of rich farmland are on the sites of ancient beaver ponds, on land created by beavers.

Many country boys know how to make a swimming hole. The usual method is to build a small dam across a stream with logs, brush, and rocks and fill the cracks with mud and sod. Beavers work in much the same way, using their teeth instead of a hatchet. Dams a thousand feet long have been known in our national parks, while others twenty feet thick and twelve to fourteen feet high have been measured. Out in the ponds moundlike houses with underwater entrances are built. Legend has it that those occasional beavers who live in streambanks instead of houses are engineers who had done a poor job and were driven out of the colony.

In 1920 three pairs of beavers, captured in the Adirondacks, were liberated in Bear Mountain Park, forty miles north of New York City. Today hundreds of beavers are the progeny of the original six. The change they have brought about in the park is amazing. Water-thrushes now nest near every pond and wood ducks, not found at all before the beavers came, live throughout the area. Tree swallows and crested flycatchers nest in holes in the drowned stubs which project from the still water, while red-wings sing from the sedge. Deer come to drink at the pools and muskrats now find room for their own houses. The beaver is truly the master wildlife engineer.

The beaver's small associate, the muskrat (about the size of a small cat) is probably America's most profitable fur-bearer today. Many marshes are preserved simply so they may furnish a crop of muskrats. Millions are taken each year, but so long as these animals are wisely managed as a harvest there will always be plenty of them. At the same time ducks and other marsh creatures benefit by having a place to live in which might otherwise be drained and turned into onion fields.

The wily mink, a large water-loving weasel, is the muskrat's nemesis, but it in turn is sometimes caught by the great horned owl. In nature everything must eat something else. The beaver and the muskrat are vegetarians for the most part, but the mink and otter must have meat. Both are very clever at catching frogs and fish. The otter at work is a marvel to behold. With the agility of a seal it easily outswims the fastest fish. Several times as large as a mink, it is a magnificent streamlined creature measuring four or five feet from its whiskered snout to the tip of its tapering tail. Otters are rarely seen nowadays.

Muskrat

Mink

79

Ring-necked Duck

Wood Duck

DUCKS OF THE STREAMS AND WOODED LAKES

One of the best ways to find birds, waterfowl in particular, is to put a canoe or folding boat into the current and glide downstream. When ducks are on the move, it is possible to jump a dozen species or more on some creeks, especially if there are open marshes along the margin. Wooded waters have their own special ducks, some of which are shown here.

The ring-necked duck, which looks much like a scaup or "bluebill" when it is on the water, can be identified by its black back and, in flight, by its broad gray wing stripe. During recent years when there has been so much concern about the decline of some of the waterfowl it has been good to see one that seems to be increasing, actually spreading its range. A nesting bird of wooded lakes just east of the prairies in Canada, the ring-neck has recently spread eastward to Maine and has even got a foothold in Newfoundland. All this is reflected in the numbers which now come through in migration. On certain ponds we can always find little flocks, diving deep for water plants, but we search in vain for them on nearby ponds which look equally good. Only the ring-necks themselves know the reason.

No picture, no matter how well done, can do justice to the bizarre pattern and deep iridescent coloring of the male wood duck. Many believe it to be the most beautiful duck in the world, but others contend it is almost too highly colored and that its close relative, the mandarin duck of China, is really more handsome. Paddling downstream, the canoeist frightens pairs of "woodies" which flee through the trees shrieking whoo-eek! As if by some inviolate rule of duck courtesy the females always precede the males. They maneuver skillfully through the timber and have no difficulty alighting on horizontal limbs high up, a most unducklike act. Unducklike too is their habit of nesting in old pileated woodpecker holes and other tree hollows. They can even be induced to use large boxes of the squirrel house type, or kegs. At the Chautauqua Wildlife Refuge in Illinois where hundreds of wood-duck boxes have been put up, a high percentage have been used. For years a controversy raged as to how the duck-lings got to the water. Some swore that the female carried them on her back; motion pictures finally settled the argu-ment, showing that the fluffy babies pop out of the hole one by one, and bounce on the ground when they land! One observer saw a brood of babies jump twenty-two feet onto a concrete sidewalk, yet none were injured.

The wood duck, nesting in farm country throughout the East, was too vulnerable to make a satisfactory game bird. It was well on its way out of the picture when complete protection was given it in 1918. Now there are many again, and although their hunting is not encouraged, a single bird is allowed in the gunner's bag in some states.

The smart-looking hooded mergan-ser (lower right) also has the tree-nest-ing habit and for this reason sometimes competes with the wood duck for the same hole. The wood duck usually wins. In the experience of most of us the hooded merganser is one of the scarcer ducks, but we can always expect a few on certain ponds and creeks dur-ing migration. The males have collap-sible crests which can be raised in a fan or compressed.

Flying in line formation, low over the water, mergansers follow the wind-ing courses of the streams. All three species of this subfamily are fish eaters, outswimming their finny prey under-water where they seize them with their narrow bills, which are lined with tiny teeth. The American merganser or goosander is the biggest of the three fish ducks, and, on fresh water, the commonest. In the latitude of the Great Lakes it is the most typical win-ter duck, remaining on the rivers and lakes as long as there is any open water.

American Merganser

Hooded Merganser

81

Common Loon

Horned Grebe

BIRDS OF THE LAKES AND BAYS

Out on the broad waters of the bays, reservoirs, and open lakes flights of waterfowl come in during migration, but, for the most part, they are not the same kinds that drop into the marshes. They are ducks like the canvasback, scaup, redhead, golden-eye, and bufflehead (pages 108 and 109), deepwater ducks that dive for a living. For convenience we call them bay ducks. But there are other birds besides these on the lakes and bays. Herring and ring-billed gulls give life to the blue water, and common terns (page 110) skim and dip like large silvery swallows.

Loons, long and low, cruise like avian submarines on the rippled surface, ready to submerge in a flash. When they come through in spring many are in the plumage shown above, but some are in plainer garb, dark above and light below, for it takes nearly four years to attain the checkerboard pattern (they lose it again each winter). Most loons do not tarry long but continue on to Maine, the Adirondacks, Minnesota, or Canada, where they resort to lakes deep in the forest.

There on a boggy island or perhaps on a muskrat house, they lay their two big eggs. On such a lake their wild laughter echoes against the dark shores and campers are startled by weird yodelings at night. In what seems to be some sort of game, parties of loons often race across the open water, laugh and jeer wildly at each other, then race again.

Little groups of horned grebes which have wintered along the coast also stop during April and May in their trek to the lakes of Canada. Breasting the cold waves, and diving, they look like little ducks with pointed bills and golden ear tufts. When they return, along toward winter, they no longer have the ear tufts and are dark above and white below, suggesting miniature loons.

Long ago nearly every lake or bay must have had its pair of bald eagles. But today many Americans have never seen their national bird. It is still quite common along the west coast of Florida and in the Chesapeake-Potomac area near Washington, and a few pairs reside here and there along the coast of Maine, around the Great Lakes and

82

elsewhere, but in many states in the union not a single bald eagle's eyrie is known. However, it is possible to see bald eagles in spring or summer even in states like Massachusetts where none are known to breed. Charles Broley, the "eagle man," who has banded over 1100 young eagles in Florida has found that all his eagles wander north in late spring and that some even reach Canada.

Bald Eagle

Today the bald eagle is protected by federal law, but it makes a big tempting target, so some are still shot. This is regrettable because the bald eagle is not destructive. It will catch a crippled duck when it can, but ninety per cent of its food is fish, usually dead fish which it finds along the shore. It sometimes highjacks the osprey, swooping down from above until the "fish hawk" drops its catch.

Nesting ospreys are gone from the British Isles, but we shall probably always have ours because nearly everyone likes the big fish hawk. At Cape May, New Jersey, farmers erect cartwheels on tall poles to induce them to nest. Hundreds live along the coast, but their distribution is spotty. There are said to be 200 nests on Gardiner's Island, New York. Inland ospreys have not fared as well. Their population has declined at least seventy-five per cent because they have been destroyed at fish hatcheries.

Osprey

The kingfisher is also tempted by the small fry in the hatcheries, but many caretakers who do not relish the constant killing of these attractive birds now screen the runs or use wires and other devices to discourage them. However, along the streams and about the lakes we do not begrudge the kingfisher his catch. The fish, after all, are his as well as ours.

Belted Kingfisher

Brown Trout

FISHES OF THE BROOKS AND STREAMS

A stream, clean and sweet, is not entirely H_2O. Even the most sparkling New England brook, rambling over polished stones, has some mineral content in its waters. A creek draining the limestone ridges of West Virginia is likely to have a milky cast while one in Quebec might have the look of pale tea, colored by the vegetation of the bogs from which it springs. But these are healthy waters, not like the muddy brown creeks whose silt from eroded fields excludes the sunlight. Sadder still are those streams which carry the poisons of civilization—streams into which have been dumped the industrial waste and filth of the cities along the banks— polluted streams in which even the coarsest fish can scarcely survive. However, "men may come and men may go," and such brooks and rivers can be restored from biologically barren streams to waters fit for trout. Their restoration is not just an esthetic principle, but an economic one. Millions of men spend millions of dollars every year seeking relaxation by whipping the riffles for the spirited fish shown here jumping for mayflies.

No two specialists agree how many kinds of trout there are. One authority has listed 41 varieties in the United States and Canada; another believes there are at least 187. This disparity in numbers is because many kinds are not full species, merely local populations confined to a few streams; fish that

Brook Trout

84

Rainbow Trout

Brook Stickleback

differ only in minor details from their cousins in neighboring streams. Some authorities believe these should be given special names, others do not. Besides this, fish hatcheries have complicated matters by crossing different trout.

The original trout of most eastern streams is the brook trout, the lovely shy fish that lives in clear cool brooks, snatching up the insects that fall into the pools. It is this habit that has led to the invention of fly fishing, considered by millions of Isaac Walton followers as the highest form of their sport. Fly-tying has become an art, and the variety of flies devised from feathers is infinite.

In the North, the brook trout often enters the cold sea water. There it takes on a silvery look. In the South it never reaches the sea, but wanders downstream from the hills only as far as the flow of cool water (not exceeding 68° F.). A five-pound brook trout is considered large, but giants weighing fourteen pounds or more are on record.

The brown trout of Europe was set free in America in 1883. Although it seems to drive the native brook trout out of some streams, particularly the warmer ones, many fishermen proclaim that it was a great day for trout-fishing when this wily fish was introduced. It is gamier than the guillible brook trout,

more difficult to catch, and suspicious of even the choicest flies. For this reason it is harder to "fish out" a stream in which brown trout live. Although a seven- or eight-pound brown trout is a good-sized fish, monsters of forty pounds have been caught.

The rainbow trout of the West was brought in cans across the great divide and dumped into eastern streams as early as 1880. Now this handsome fish with the broad pink stripe is familiar to anglers in many parts of the world. Like the brown trout it can live in warmer water than the brook trout (up to 80°). Often after it is stocked in mountain streams it disappears, having migrated to warmer, broader waters, which it seems to prefer.

Except for the minnows they sometimes use for bait, sports fishermen are scarcely conscious of the many tiny non-game fish that live in the streams and lakes. Some are valuable controllers of mosquito larvæ. One of the most fascinating of these midgets is the brook stickleback, a little fellow less than 2½ inches long which builds a tiny hollow nest, open at both ends, in which the eggs are laid. These the male fiercely defends. He is a great fighter, using his sharp spines in combat with rival sticklebacks.

Crappie

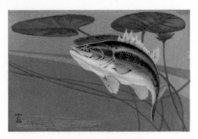

Largemouth Bass

Bullhead

Channel Cat

FISHES OF THE RIVERS

Kingfishers need no rods or reels. Neither do bitterns, mink, snapping turtles, or giant water bugs. All take their share of little fish. So do many of the fish themselves. Big bass often eat little bass.

Fish are prolific. A brook trout might lay as many as 5000 eggs. But, as a brook can support only a certain "poundage," many small fry must be weeded out so that others will have a chance to grow. Otherwise they will remain runts which might never attain catchable size before they die of disease or old age. Biologists, therefore, believe that fish predators such as the king-fisher are actually essential to good fishing. So we do not nurse a grudge against them. To have more fish we must improve the stream itself.

Farm fishponds are becoming quite popular. The crappie is easily trans-planted and thrives in the rather warm water of these ponds. This pretty little bass which lives in rivers and ponds from the Great Lakes to the Gulf of Mexico goes by a long list of names, such as "calico bass," "papermouth," "strawberry bass," etc. Its cousin the largemouth black bass is the most pop-ular game fish of all, according to a vote taken among sportsmen by the National Wildlife Federation. In the north a five-pounder is a large one, but in the warmer, more sluggish waters of Flo-rida it sometimes tips the scales at twenty.

The catfish, a large family, range from little fellows called madtoms, which hide under stones and inflict painful wounds with their venomous spines, to the familiar bullheads and

American Shad

Alligator Gar

Fresh-water Drum

Bowfin

big channel cats. All have smooth scaleless skins and "cat's whiskers" or barbels which they use in feeling for food on the muddy bottom. The bullhead, the favorite of farm boys, is among the most delicious of all panfish, particularly in colder water. Although most catfish like sluggish streams with muddy bottoms, the channel cat, the most streamlined member of the family, prefers large swift-flowing rivers. It often congregates in the fast water downstream from power dams.

The shad is one of the anadromous fish which spend most of their lives at sea but swarm into the fresh-water rivers to spawn. When the shad are moving upstream men line the riverbanks to intercept them. Those females which successfully run the gauntlet may lay as many as 150,000 eggs each. Dams across the rivers and pollution have sadly depleted some of the old shad runs.

The alligator gar, the largest of the gars, lives in southern rivers north to the Ohio. An armor-plated dreadnaught, which raids schools of lesser fish, it might reach a length of ten feet and a weight of 100 pounds.

The fresh-water drum or "sheepshead" makes the strange croaking or purring sound peculiar to the family (most species live in salt water). Apparently the giants have all been caught long ago, because bones found in Indian kitchen middens indicate they may have reached 200 pounds. Today in Lake Erie, where they are caught commercially, a 10-pounder is exceptional.

The bowfin with its long wavy dorsal fin and black eye spot near its tail isn't much of a food fish but puts up a savage fight when hooked. A rather primitive fish, found from the St. Lawrence to Texas, it can live in foul muddy water, or even in a half-dried puddle.

Smallmouth Bass

Yellow Perch

Rock Bass

Bluegill Sunfish

FISHES OF THE LAKES

It is not so easy as you might think to identify some fish. Anglers recognize subtle distinctions between varieties in their own lakes, and have names for them, colorful names that might be quite different from those used for the same fish in the next watershed. The experts identify their fish by systematically counting scales or the number of fin rays. In the Great Lakes district, 233 species and subspecies have been catalogued. In Florida, bounded by the sea and honeycombed with teeming lakes, there must be several times that many. Many of these are little fellows of course; minnows, "shiners," and "mosquito fish," of little interest to the average angler except as bait.

The smallmouth black bass is the fisherman's delight, pound for pound one of the sportiest of all fish. Its mouth is only *relatively* smaller than that of a largemouth black bass (not extending beyond the eye) and it is finer scaled, but otherwise the two look much alike. The smallmouth likes colder water with sandy or rocky bottom. A seven-pounder is a large fish but the line record is fourteen.

The yellow perch, striped like a coon's tail, is a slimmer fish than a bass or sunfish but lives in many of the same lakes and ponds where the water is quiet and the bottom muddy. A perch a foot long, or more than a pound in weight, is a very large one, but one caught many years ago at Bordentown, New Jersey, weighed over four pounds.

The rock bass with its big ruby-red-

Sunfish

Lake Trout

Eastern Pickerel

Whitefish

eye is a favorite among the "panfish," the small game fish that make up the bulk of fishing on ponds and lakes. A big rock bass may weigh well over a pound. It lives in clear lakes and rocky streams throughout much of the eastern United States, and is particularly numerous in the upper Mississippi Valley.

There are many sunfishes, but the one that has been nicknamed the "pumpkinseed" is the boys favorite. Although only four to six inches long (never more than eight) it is so scrappy that it would be rated a top game fish if it were only larger. The male builds a nest among the weeds, lines it with rootlets and gravel, and maintains a harem. Should you put your hand in the water near his nursery he will attack. The common sunfish or "pumpkinseed" has a red spot on its ear flaps

while the bluegill (lower left), has a black one. Bluegills are larger, sometimes reaching a foot in length and a weight of one and one half pounds. Most sunfish are more brightly hued than the bluegill, but their colors, almost as evanescent as the rainbow, come and go.

The slim wolfish-looking pickerel which averages about two feet in length is much sought by ice fishermen in the North. It is abundant in the weedy creeks and ponds of the Deep South as well.

In cold deepwater lakes from Maine and the Great Lakes northward the big lake trout lurks. Drab with light flecks, it commonly runs to ten pounds or more and has been known to reach a hundred. The lake trout and whitefish are two of the chief fish netted by the commercial fisheries of the Great

Great Northern Pike

Lake Sturgeon

Lakes. Both have been so exploited that the once enormous supply is rapidly running out. The take of whitefish has been worth several million dollars a year but unless the harvest is drastically regulated, a valuable wildlife resource will be lost.

Fishing is big business. Commercial fish and fish products mean more than a billion dollars a year to the coffers of our country. At least another billion changes hands for boats, tackle, guides, etc., in the pursuit of game fish. Fifteen and a half million fishing licenses were issued in 1949. Here is a renewable natural resource of the first magnitude, worth taking care of.

Five hundred hatcheries turn out fish by the million, but this method alone is not the answer to good fishing. I once saw several thousand small trout (5 to 7 inches long) dumped into a dammed-up pool in the desert mountains. Many men who "waited for the season to open" got their limit in the first two hours and by the second morning every fish had been caught. It reminded me of the toy fishponds with cardboard fish which we used to play games with.

Ira Gabrielson, director of the Wildlife Management Institute, points out that good fish management must follow the same two cardinal principles of game management: (1) to take care of

the environment, and (2) to limit the harvest to the crop produced.

The real giants among fresh-water fish—record-breaking fish—become fewer as the years go on, but there are still many large fellows in some of the lakes. The great northern pike might grow nearly as long as a canoe paddle and weigh 40 pounds (the line record is 46 pounds). It is found in cool lakes all the way from New England and the Great Lakes through Canada to Alaska. Very voracious like the others of its family, the pickerel and the muskellunge, it lives off the lesser fish, darting at them suddenly and snatching them up in its scoop-shovel jaws.

The muskellunge, king of all the fresh-water game fish, grows even larger than the pike. There is a record of a female, caught in 1902 by the Wisconsin Conservation Department that weighed 102 pounds. The line record is 64 pounds. Casting with a plug, or trolling with a spinner behind the boat still brings large muskies to the surface, but because the big ones are getting scarcer some sportsmen release their prizes so they might catch them another time.

The lake sturgeon, a giant that has been known to exceed seven feet in length and 300 pounds in weight, was once abundant in the Great Lakes, particularly in Lake Erie. Costly caviar

Chautauqua Muskellunge

Landlocked Salmon

Wall-eyed Pike

made from the roe, incited commercial netters to take so many of these armor-plated monsters that the species was in danger of extinction. Now with protective legislation it is believed to be making a slow return. Its salt-water cousin, the Atlantic sturgeon, has had a similar history.

The landlocked salmon is really a form of the Atlantic salmon—one that became isolated long ago in lakes in Maine and the Maritime Provinces and did not return to the sea. Whereas the Atlantic salmon has all but disappeared along some parts of the coast, its inland relative has prospered (with some help from the fisheries) and is now distributed widely throughout the Northeast.

The wall-eyed pike, with its strange milky eyes, is perhaps as numerous as any of the larger fresh-water game fish. It is so numerous in parts of Lake Erie that it has been profitable to net it commercially there. Millions of pounds are taken each year. Many fishermen vote it their favorite eating fish. Prolific, a large female might lay as many as 900,000 eggs, but the small fry start cutting down competition before they are two weeks old by eating each other! An average wall-eye weighs four pounds, but a large one may exceed twenty.

THE SWAMPS AND FRESH MARSHES

What is the difference between a swamp and a marsh? If we use the terms loosely, as so many do, we probably draw no distinction, employing either word to mean any piece of low muddy ground which is soggy to walk on or partly covered with water. But if we are to be accurate, a swamp is a wet place dominated by *trees and shrubs*. A marsh, on the other hand, is a wet *treeless* area dominated by grass, sedge, and cattails.

Swamps and marshes are the half-way point in succession, land being created where there had been water. In fact a marsh often turns into a swamp as time goes on. It is a gradual process; first bushes invade the cattails, later trees get a foothold.

Climb a tall tree at the edge of the marsh. Acres of waving cattails spread into the distance, ponds glint in the sunlight, and half-hidden streams connect the little pools with the big ones.

There are sure to be birds, for no environment has a higher density than a good swamp or marsh. Red-winged blackbirds sway on the tips of the willows. Marsh wrens chatter in the reeds; rails grunt and whinny.

There is always something going on. Southern marshes have the most herons and other big waders—the "glamour birds." Midwestern and far-western marshes support the bulk of the nesting ducks; together with the Canadian and Alaskan marshes they are the waterfowl nurseries of the continent.

Unfortunately for wildlife, between 80,000,000 and 100,000,000 acres of land have been drained in the United States for agriculture alone. Millions more have been drained to control mosquitoes. Thus, millions of acres of water have been hurried off the land before their time, hurried to the sea before they have given enough service to plants, birds, beasts, and men. Each day new plans are made somewhere in our country to drain another lake, swamp, or marsh. This cannot go on forever. There will soon be no swamps or marshes left.

Water conservationists are aware that drainage lowers the underground water table. When snow or rain falls to earth, some of it sinks into the ground. Penetrating the subsoil and porous rock it eventually reaches the great underground reservoirs where water is stored. The upper level of this is called the *water table*. Where it reaches the surface in hollows of the land, ponds are formed, or swamps and marshes. Water seeks its own level. Thus when a marsh is ditched and the water is sent hurrying on its way, the whole water table is lowered. Then many plants can no longer reach the reserve of moisture with their roots, and men must dig deeper wells. Because natural laws have been ignored great water shortages now exist in some places.

Sportsmen know that if the marshes go the ducks will go. They have come to regard the engineer who "reclaims" land and straight-jackets streams as the greatest enemy of their sport. Some of the lands which have been drained and turned to the plow have since proven submarginal, quite hopeless for a farmer to make a profit on, and much more useful for a wildlife crop such as muskrats or waterfowl. So at great expense (for the second time) they have been dyked, flooded, and returned to their original condition. The great Malheur marsh in Oregon is a famous example.

All the hunting regulations in the world won't do the ducks much good if their nesting grounds continue to be reduced. When a duck tries to nest in a ditched marsh the cards are stacked against it. Food is scarce and the ditches are a trap for the babies, which cannot climb the steep sides. Fires sweep the dried-out sedge, roasting eggs and ducklings. Where water is deficient or wanting, epidemics of *botulism* or "duck sickness" sometimes break out and waterfowl perish in appalling numbers.

Those among us who simply enjoy watching wild things and cannot live without them know that ditching a marsh means the end for the muskrats, rails, bitterns, marsh wrens, and gallinules. But, you may ask, don't they just go elsewhere? Of course they do, but wherever they go there is competition. Marshes are already carrying full capacity. Someone must lose out somewhere. So, when a marsh is drained, the ten pairs of red-wings, thirty pairs of marsh wrens, twelve pairs of swamp sparrows, and twenty pairs of ducks which nest there are eliminated. Perhaps not the identical individuals, but the equivalent number, in due course, somewhere. To quote an apt simile: "A habitat is like a house. If the family dies another family can move in; but if the house burns down, no one can live there."

Our federal government through its refuge program (see page 102) hopes to preserve and develop enough marshes which can act as breeding reservoirs, so that there will always be enough waterfowl to fill the flyways of the continent. Should you live near one of these Fish and Wildlife Service refuges, pay it a visit. You will see not only waterfowl, but more birds and other wildlife than you will in any other spot for miles around.

Fringed Gentian

FLOWERS OF
THE LOW WET PLACES

To a person who likes his land-scapes manicured, a swamp may seem unsightly. But to anyone who loves the outdoors, the swamps, the bogs, and the marshes are among the most attractive spots of all. Because they are hard to get into they retain their wild-ness and have an aura of mystery.

Many of our rarest and most lovely flowers bloom in the bogs where you must pay the penalty of wet feet if you would find them. Others, like some of those shown on these two pages, prefer the firmer ground at the edges of swamps, or the banks of streams.

The fringed gentian, which the poets have made famous, comes into bloom in September and October, after most other flowers have gone to seed. Then its misty banners unfurl in a last colorful salute to the autumn country-side. Late butterflies and bees fly from blossom to blossom, insuring cross-pol-lination, but ants are unwanted, hence the value of the fringe on each petal which keeps them from climbing aboard. After the seed pods form, the plants die. It takes two years for the new plants to come into bloom. Beauti-ful as they are, do not pick them or transplant them to your garden (they are very difficult to grow anyway). Gentians need protection.

The closed gentian, or bottle gen-tian, which comes into bloom at the end of summer seems like a locked vault, designed to guard its pollen. However, the bumblebee, with its broad shoulders, pushes its way into

Closed Gentian

Spotted Touch-me-not

94

the valvelike opening, rifles the treasure, and goes with its burden of golden dust to the next reluctant blossom.

Delicately hung, like jeweled ear pendants, the jewelweed or snapweed grows in thickets along the banks of brooks and at the edges of the swamps. In late summer its spotted orange blossoms are a favorite of hummingbirds which dart from bush to bush, squeaking excitedly. Touch-me-not, another name it bears, is very appropriate when the small tubular seed pods mature. At the merest touch they explode with a tiny pop, scattering seeds in all directions.

Bogs where the soil is acid are the homes of many native orchids. There are scores of species in America. Many are inconspicuous and drab, but some, the lady's slippers in particular, can hold their own with the most flamboyant tropical varieties. The showy lady's slipper, the state flower of Minnesota, is without doubt the most spectacular of all our native orchids. Few who see it can resist picking it, so today it has become quite rare, except in the wilder sections. Even there it hides behind a screen of ferns or bushes and you must search to find it.

To a real flower lover it is as wrong to transplant a wild orchid or a gentian to the garden as it is to cage a cardinal or a wood thrush. To pick them is virtually to destroy them, because they do not reproduce easily. However, if one must have wild bouquets there are many flowers like the prolific jewelweed which can be picked freely.

The exquisite Virginia bluebell which demurely nods its bells in early spring in the wooded river bottoms is always a temptation to pick, but spare it; pick a handful of violets instead.

Showy Lady's Slipper

Virginia Bluebell

95

Giant St. Johnswort

Royal Fern

One wonders how deer, cattle, and other animals which eat vegetation can avoid the many plants whose leaves are poisonous, plants such as the blue flag and marsh marigold, shown opposite. Yet, most grazing animals seem to know instinctively what not to eat. The leaves of the St. Johnsworts, a large family of bushy-stamened yellow flowers, are supposed to be poisonous, but the seeds are palatable, so birds often eat them. The great St. Johnswort, shown here, grows along streams in the northern states, where it is the largest of its tribe, often reaching a height of five feet. The common St. Johnswort, a smaller species, can often be found in vacant lots.

Many ferns like the ruch humus and the moisture of the swamps, and unroll their fiddleheads as soon as spring gets underway. The royal fern, above, looks like no other. Its beautiful clusters, sometimes so dense that birds can nest in them, decorate streamsides from Newfoundland to Florida and Texas.

The skunk cabbage is the first spring flower in the northern states, pushing its homely hooded blossoms through the thawing soil as soon as the snow melts. Many people despise it because the large leaves, which unfold later, have a rank skunklike odor, but city people, unfamiliar with this lowly plant, are captivated by pictures of it, often thinking it some strange kind of tropical orchid until they are told its name.

Often growing with the skunk cabbage in the same wet spots are spectacular displays of cowslips or marsh marigolds. Their yellow blossoms look like clusters of large buttercups. The round leaves are poisonous to cattle, but make delicious greens for the table when cooked.

The blue flag iris lends its deep royal blue to the wet meadows and marshes from Newfoundland to Florida. Its swordlike leaves and its roots, like those of the marsh marigold and St. Johnsworts, are also toxic to grazing animals and are left strictly alone by them, so this regal beauty has little to offer wildlife—except nectar for the bees. So constituted that self-fertilization is impossible, it lures passing insects to perform the miracle of cross-pollination.

But beauty is its own excuse for being. What more would we require from the swamp rose mallow (upper right) whose gorgeous hibiscus-like blossoms, five to seven inches across, glow in late summer in brackish marshes along the coast? Standing as tall as a man, the rose mallow is a not too distant relative of the familiar hollyhock of the garden.

Marsh Marigold

Swamp Rose Mallow

Skunk Cabbage

Larger Blue Flag

Yellow Pond-lily

Sweet-scented White Water-lily

American Lotus

FLOWERS OF THE PONDS

Every boy who goes fishing knows at least two or three of these flowers. They grow where the sunfish bite best, their roots deep in the mud and their shining faces emerging above the still water.

The yellow pond-lily grows in almost every good frog pond from the Gulf of St. Lawrence to the Gulf of Mexico. Because cattle like to wade belly-deep and pull up the long succulent stems it is often called the cow lily. Few plants have more food value for wildlife. Ducks gobble the seeds; moose, deer, muskrats, and beavers eat its roots and stems. Even Indians collected the sweet rootstocks in the old days. At summer's end the leathery leaves and the slippery stems die and disintegrate into the mud. They and the other pond plants are the pioneer soil builders, the first in the long succession of plants which slowly build land where there has been water.

The sweet-scented white water-lily seems choosier than the yellow pond-lily. It does not grow in every pond, but when it finds the right pool or cove it covers its surface with hundreds of floating platter-shaped leaves and puts forth its snowy blooms to attract the bees and flower flies. Small fish lurk in the shade of the leaves and probably find plenty of food there. Notice when you turn over a leaf how slimy with algæ and tiny water animals it is on its pinkish underside.

The American lotus, very local in the North, is much more often seen in the

98

South where immense lotus gardens flourish in some of the rivers and lakes. The huge pads or shields, more than a foot across (sometimes two feet), do not float but are held proudly aloft on their strong stems. The creamy or pale yellowish blossoms are double the expanse of those of the water-lily, almost as large as the pink blossoms of the Egyptian lotus which is sometimes grown in aquatic gardens.

The pickerelweed, arrowhead, and some of the other pond plants that stand at the water's edge remind us of those other long-legged waders, the herons, bitterns, and rails. Standing on slender stalks, the pickerelweed is known by its shiny arrow-shaped leaf and hyacinth-like spike of blue flowers. Its name comes from the legend, perhaps partly true, that the pickerel lays its eggs in the shallow water where it grows.

At the edges of boggy northern lakes the water arum (lower right) sends up its arrow-shaped leaves and calla-like blossoms. Often called the "wild calla," it belongs to the same family (Araceæ) as the calla lily of Eastertime. The skunk cabbage and jack-in-the-pulpit are also relatives.

Most of the plants shown here, and many others not shown, which grow in the ponds and about their edges are valuable to wildlife—either their seeds or their roots are eaten; often the leaves themselves. Not so the water hyacinth. Although gorgeous to behold, as masses of bladder-buoyed plants drift on the current like fairy gardens, it is of little use to wildlife. An invader from Brazil, it now chokes our southern rivers, and *millions* have been spent to clear it from boat channels and harbors.

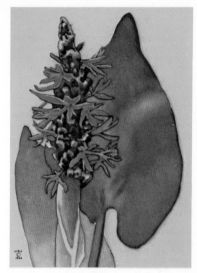

Pickerelweed

Water Hyacinth

Water Arum

99

Leopard Frog

Green Frog

Bullfrog

FROGS AND TURTLES
OF THE PONDS AND MARSHES

The frogs sang their songs ages before the birds did. They were here first. Frogs, toads, and salamanders are *amphibians*, the first class of animals to climb out of ancient seas onto the land. "Amphibious," a word of Greek origin, means "leading a double life."

Some frogs, such as our little "spring peepers," have voices that are almost birdlike, but most are more guttural. Nevertheless, these sounds that pipe from a hundred throats on evenings in spring are cosmic music—love songs of the swamp. The ardent males puff out their throats like bubble gum, and bleat, trill, or croak, depending on their kind, until a female is won. When Arthur A. Allen and Paul Kellogg of Cornell made their sound recordings of North American birds, so many frogs intruded their harmonies onto the sound track that they decided to record all of the eastern frogs while they were about it. An album of these recordings, including the songs of twenty-six species of frogs and toads, has been published by the Comstock Publishing Company of Ithaca, New York, under the title "Voices of the Night." Now you can learn these elusive voices right in your own living room.

Leopard frog is a good descriptive name for the spotted fellow at the upper left, but because it wanders far and wide in the long damp grass, many prefer to call it the meadow frog. Not only do herons and bitterns spear it when they can, but fishermen catch it for bait, epicures fry the delicious legs in batter, and biology students learn from it their first lessons in anatomy. Fortunately, the large clusters of eggs that suggest masses of tapioca insure future tadpoles and, later, froglets. Incidentally, frogs lay their eggs in clusters, toads in strings.

The green frog, which lacks the distinct spots of the leopard, can be found in almost any ditch where there is water. Its single croak sounds like plucking a loose string on some instrument.

The bullfrog, granddaddy of them all, is the one that sings "jug-a-rum" in a deep musical bass. So sought after by frog catchers that it has become scarce in many places, closed seasons and bag-limits have become inevitable. The largest bullfrog on record tipped the scales at three and one-half pounds.

There is no purer sound than the long sweet trill of a toad on a still night in May. One would not expect this stubby-legged gnome (lower right) to be so musical. Hopping about the garden at dusk, toads eat incredible numbers of insects, snapping them up with their long sticky tongues. No songbird is more beneficial.

Although turtles lead an "amphibious" life they are a step or so further up the evolutionary ladder—reptiles that have found a way to live inside their own ribs. Protected by such armor they live long lives, providing they survive babyhood. Hungry skunks and coons dig up the parchment-skinned eggs. The spotted turtle with its yellow spots, and the painted turtle with its red border design, both love to bask in the warm sun on the edge of the pond, but they feel safer on an old log out in the water. There they may stack up two or three deep if there isn't room enough for everybody.

101

Spotted Turtle

Painted Turtle

American Toad

Gadwall

Green-winged Teal

Pintail

Shoveller

DUCKS OF THE FRESH MARSHES

All of the ducks on these two pages are dabblers. They do not dive like the mergansers or other deepwater ducks; there is no need to, for their living comes from the marsh. They reach the pondweeds and succulent roots of water plants merely by dabbling or by standing on their heads in the shallow water. When they fly they do not skitter or patter like heavily laden seaplanes taking off, the way diving ducks do, but spring straight into the air, then level off.

The marsh ducks are the ones which furnish the two million duck-hunters of our country with most of their sport. Naturally, such a valuable national resource must be guarded. The United States Fish and Wildlife Service assumes this responsibility. Each year, after careful study, it pegs the bag-limit so that sportsmen may crop the harvest but not cut into "seed stock." Enough ducks must return to the nesting marshes in the spring so that a new crop will fill the flyways in the fall.

To keep tabs on the numbers half a dozen flyway biologists live with the ducks throughout the year, count them, and follow them on their travels. Then there is the annual winter duck inventory in which more than 3000 observers take part. Game management agents, wardens, biologists, bird watchers, forest service and park service men, all count the wintering flocks. Even navy blimps, army planes, and coast guard boats are put to use.

There are over 200 federal refuges in which waterfowl nest or spend the win-

102

ter. These refuges which cover more than 3,500,000 acres are financed in part by the sale of the famous "duck stamps" (each duck hunter buys one for two dollars). Canada has also set aside millions of acres. Even so, the ducks have their ups and downs. They dropped to an all-time low of 27,000,-000 in 1935. They were gradually restored to 125,000,000 by 1944, slumped to 54,000,000 in 1947, recovered somewhat, then slumped again during 1949.

Ducks are no more difficult to identify than songbirds; the males, at least, have good field marks. As for the drab females, identify them by the company they keep. The gadwall (upper left) is the only marsh duck with a white speculum (the patch on the hind edge of the wing). The green-winged teal, the smallest duck, flashes an iridescent green speculum and a green patch on its brown head. The blue-winged teal (page 9) is marked with a white crescent on its face, and has blue shoulders. The shoveller has a chestnut belly and a spoon-shaped bill, twice as wide at the tip as it is at the base.

The graceful pintail is known by the white line on its neck as well as by its needle tail. The black duck, most familiar marsh duck in the Northeast, is sooty with flashing white linings to its dark wings. The mallard, perhaps the most numerous duck in the world, has a green head and a white neck ring, exactly like the puddle mallards in every park. For the field marks of all ducks as they appear on the water and also their flight patterns overhead be sure to see the plates in *A Field Guide to the Birds*. With this book, or *A Field Guide to Western Birds*, you can learn to tell most ducks when they are a quarter of a mile away.

Black Duck

Mallard

103

Red-winged Blackbird

Marsh Hawk

Wilson's Snipe

Florida Gallinule

OTHER BIRDS OF
THE MARSHES

No habitat has more birds than a good marsh. The hidden pools, channels, and patches of cattails are the haven of birds as diverse as great blue herons with a wingspan of six feet and tiny marsh wrens scarcely more than four inches long. Censuses often show as many as fifteen or twenty nesting birds per acre in the summertime, and far more than that when the migrating swallows, blackbirds, and waterfowl come through.

Everyone should know the red-winged blackbird because it breeds in every state in the Union. In the North it arrives with the first wave of migrants in spring, along with the robins and bluebirds. Shortly thereafter the males make themselves doubly conspicuous by monopolizing the best perches in the swamp and by puffing out their scarlet epaulets each time they sing *konk-er-eeeeee*. If a crow or a hawk passes by, they see it on its way, darting like little dive bombers from above. The marsh hawk or harrier (left) is used to this, though, and merely glides along, quartering back and forth, looking for whatever small furry fare it can find. Unlike most other hawks, when gliding it holds its wings above the horizontal in a vulture-like *dihedral*. This and the white patch on its rump are the harrier's marks.

Wilson's snipe probe the oozy margins but "freeze" when we come slogging through the sedge. We seldom get a glimpse of these long-nosed birds before they hurtle themselves into the air and zigzag away. Most snipe spend the summer in Canada's cool bogs.

There they forget their shy habits and advertise themselves by "winnowing" high in the air. Cruising almost out of sight, they zoom in steep dives, producing the unearthly sound so characteristic of June days in the North.

Florida gallinules croak, cluck, and carry on like complaining hens from behind the wall of cattails in the marsh, but by patiently watching we might see one swimming across a deep pool, nodding its head with each stroke. It is a ducklike bird with a red bill. Rails are even harder to see than gallinules as they slip through the reeds. The Virginia rail talks aplenty; it "kicks and grunts" but to most people it remains a mysterious voice in the marsh. It would rather run than trust its wings, and only when cornered at the edge of a ditch will it fly, legs dangling, to the nearest cover. The Virginia rail is small, near the size of a quail or meadowlark. If you see a larger one that looks like it, but large as a pullet, it is a king rail.

The bittern, big and brown, also tries the "freezing" trick. Standing motionless, bill pointed skyward, its streaked pattern makes perfect camouflage against the reeds. In spring, from some hidden spot deep in the marsh, we hear its hollow "pumping"—*oong-ka-choonk, oong - ka - choonk, oong - ka - choonk*.

Young night herons look much like bitterns but are not so rich a brown and lack the black wing tips. Both they and the adults, handsome with their white breasts, may be seen standing motionless along the channels, but they are much more in evidence at dusk when their flat *quok* sounds overhead as they return from the groves where they spend the day.

Virginia Rail

American Bittern

Black-crowned Night Heron

THE COAST AND THE SEA

Ask anyone who flies. He will tell you that there is a lot of water in this world. To be precise, for every square mile of land there are about two and a half square miles of ocean.

The sea is the mother of us all. It is the medium which first nurtured life before amphibians crawled onto terra firma. Even today there is a far greater abundance of life beneath its restless surface than exists on shore. The fabulous creatures which live there vary in size from miscroscopic forms, invisible to our eyes, to blue whales, a hundred feet long, weighing 300,000 pounds. Much of what goes on in the shadowy depths is unknown to us. William Beebe, who in 1934 descended a "half mile down" (3028 feet, to be exact) in a steel spheroid which he called the *bathysphere*, brought back fantastic tales of what he saw. At different levels he encountered new communities of marine creatures, until in the blue-black deep he could discern only rows and spots of light, the phosphorescent ornamentation of mysterious plankton and fish. One wonders what he might have found had he been able to descend still further. A fish has actually been snared at a depth of 19,800 feet, where the pressure is thousands of pounds per square inch. The ocean is very deep. If the Himalayas, the most lofty mountain range on earth, were dropped into the Philippine Trench near Mindanao, the summit of Everest itself would be covered by water more than a mile in depth.

The point where land and sea meet is at the edge of the waves—where they break upon the beach. There, at the juncture of the opposing elements, sanderlings race back and forth. Offshore the combers crash, and beyond is the unending watery void. There are fish out there and birds too, but the marine biologist knows that it is not quite as simple as that. He knows that neither fish nor birds wander willy-nilly over the ocean. They are more numerous in some parts of the sea; they follow certain currents, avoid others, and congregate where tidal rips and upwellings make the "soup" thick with plankton, the minute floating plants and animals which populate the sea water. Cold water is usually much better than warm for wildlife. This is because there is more plankton in it; a drop of a few degrees in the temperature of the water multiplies these tiny organisms a hundredfold. Many are phosphorescent, causing a glittering wake behind boats at night. Plankton is the food base, the pasturage, of everything that lives in the sea. The little fish thrive on it, and they in turn are gobbled up by the big fish and by seals and birds.

Along the Atlantic rim of our continent the coast is of two sorts. North of Cape Cod it is mostly rocky. Headlands defy the pounding surf and hundreds of rocky islands stand offshore. On the most seaward of these, gulls nest and idle seals wait out the tides.

To the south of Cape Cod lies the sand coast. Thousands of miles of smooth barrier beaches stretch all the way to the Gulf of Mexico and beyond. The beach shelf slopes slowly from the water's edge to the dunes, which are anchored in place by a scanty covering of beach grass. Behind lie the coastal thickets of bayberry and myrtle, the broad salt marshes, and mudflats interlaced with tidal creeks and channels. In the distance is the mainland.

Many of the birds, fish, and other inhabitants of the rock coast are quite different from those of the sand coasts. But some are the same. The gulls that use the battered rocks for their noisy nurseries spend the winter along the sandy beaches further south. Common terns nest on both rocks and sand.

It is among seafaring creatures that we find some of the most spectacular migrations: for example, the long journeys that eels make from their fresh-water rivers to the depths of the Sargasso Sea southeast of Bermuda where they breed. The movements of many fish are still shrouded in mystery, but we are able to watch birds, so consequently we know much more about them. Even so, we know very little about the travels of certain birds that spend much of their lives on the high seas, birds like the phalaropes and the jaegers.

The Arctic tern is the long-distance champion of all birds, traveling from the Arctic sea almost to the Antarctic, a journey which might cover as much as 11,000 miles in each direction. An aluminum band which Oliver Austin, Jr., placed on the leg of a fledgling tern in Labrador was returned less than four months later from the coast of southeast Africa 9000 miles away!

The golden plover (page 140) takes a short cut over the ocean—from Nova Scotia to South America—in traversing its 8000-mile route from the Arctic to the Argentine. For this reason we do not often see this swift-winged traveler along the coast unless a northeaster drives it in. Most shorebirds, however, take the coastal passage, following the marshes and mudflats behind the outer beaches. There they feed when the tide is low and rest back in the marsh when it is high—or travel, often so high that we fail to notice their smoky flocks against the blue. The best time for shorebirds is in August. During the dog days take your bathing suit, suntan oil, and binoculars and head for the coast.

Buffle-head

Redhead

Brant

WATERFOWL OF
THE COASTAL BAYS

During October, millions of waterfowl ride the flood of polar air which sweeps down from Canada. Many go directly south until they reach the broad marshes rimming the Gulf of Mexico. Others take a diagonal route, crossing the Appalachians, frost-touched with red and gold, and put down on the coastal bays. There, at Monomoy Point, Shinnecock Bay, Barnegat, the Susquehanna Flats, the Chesapeake, Back Bay, Pamlico Sound, and a thousand and one other bays and estuaries they are eagerly awaited by the waterfowlers, who hope that the flight is good and that many birds were raised on Canadian lakes during the previous summer.

Each of the ducks which dive on the wide waters of the bays has its field marks—at least the males have. The buffle-head (upper left), one of the smallest ducks, has a great white patch across its head. The golden-eye's mark is the round white spot in front of its eye. Duck hunters often call it the "whistler" because of the musical murmur of its wings when it races by. The ruddy duck (upper right), ruddy only in breeding plumage, can always be known by its small size, light cheeks, and dark unpatterned body.

The most typical bay duck along the entire coast is the scaup or "bluebill." Males at a distance appear "black at both ends and white in the middle." Great milling rafts of scaup often number thousands, but it is difficult to estimate them accurately because they bunch so tightly and because, when diving, a large number are out of sight at

American Golden-eye

Ruddy Duck

any one time. In the bays along the middle Atlantic coast, especially from New Jersey to North Carolina, one often sees with the scaup some larger white-backed ducks with bright rufous heads and long patrician profiles. These are canvasbacks, rated by many sportsmen the aristocrats of all ducks. Rafts of thousands may be seen in sparkling patches on the broad reaches of the Susquehanna flats or on the Chesapeake, main winter headquarters for canvasbacks on the Atlantic seaboard.

The redhead (left center), grayer than the canvasback, with a more rounded head, has not sustained its numbers as well as some of the other waterfowl. Its decline has been steady for many years until wildlife men have become worried. There are several likely reasons for this decrease. For one thing the redhead is rather gullible as ducks go, coming straight in to the decoys without looking them over first. Besides this, it seems a lax parent, often dropping its eggs in other ducks' nests as if not too enthusiastic about the responsibility of raising a family. But by far the most probable reason for the redhead's decline is that its breeding range lies almost entirely within the agricultural regions of the northern plains. Marshes have been

drained and hundreds of thousands of acres where it once nested have been put to the plow.

The brant (lower left) has been in an even tighter spot than the redhead. Until 1931 it had no difficulty maintaining its numbers. Those taken by gunners each year were within the normal increase. But in that year a biological catastrophe struck. The eelgrass (Zostera), the stringy ribbon-like water plant which makes up more than 80 per cent of the brant's food, was hit by a plague. According to Frederick C. Lincoln of the United States Fish and Wildlife Service the complete dying out of eelgrass on the Atlantic coast during 1930 and 1931 is one of the outstanding biological phenomena of modern times. So dependent had the brant become on this single item of diet that they died in great numbers and it was feared that this graceful little goose, scarcely larger than a mallard duck, would soon be but a museum piece. Biologists of the Fish and Wildlife Service, who have struggled for years to replant and restore the great beds of eelgrass, now report some success. Although it is still too early to call the battle won, eelgrass is again growing luxuriantly and the brant seems to be staging a comeback.

Common Tern

Laughing Gull

Brown Pelican

Peregrine Falcon or Duck Hawk

BIRDS OF SALT MEADOWS, BEACHES, AND MUDFLATS

As you would expect, the birds of the rock coast differ from those of the sand coast. However, the common tern (upper left) is cosmopolitan. Glinting over the surf like a large silvery swallow, it is as familiar to the lobster fishermen on the Maine Coast as it is to the summer bathers who sprawl on the sands of Atlantic City or Palm Beach. Nor is it confined to salt water. Thousands nest on sandy bars and islands in the Great Lakes. Its black cap and forked tail proclaim it a tern, but there are several other species of terns which look much like it. For these, see the color plate opposite page 134 in the *Field Guide to the Birds.*

The laughing gull, the little hooded, dark-backed gull which cries so hysterically, seldom leaves the coast or the tidal rivers unless strong storm winds carry it inland. Its populous colonies, sometimes numbering thousands of birds, are located on islands far out on the tidal marsh where armies of fiddler crabs crawl over the soft mud and clapper rails clatter from the rank sedge. Ditching of salt meadows for mosquito control is very destructive to birds such as these.

Brown pelicans, birds of ancient lineage, are part of the southern seascape. From the Carolinas to Florida, along the Gulf coast, and in California they are known to every surf caster, for these droll birds are expert surf fishermen in their own right. Spotting their quarry from the air they pull back their wings and plunge beak first. Sometimes a laughing gull is on hand to snatch

Greater Yellow-legs

Dowitcher

Ruddy Turnstone

Willet

the fish away when the pelican opens its beak to let the water drain from its collapsible pouch.

The peregrine falcon (lower left) is the famous hawk of falconry, the one flown by medieval knights and nobles. A few are still flown today by falconers. Crow-sized, with pointed wings and black mustaches, it is claimed to be the fastest bird that flies, possibly reaching a speed of two hundred miles per hour or more, on the "stoop," the plunge when it overtakes its prey. Biologists agree that the peregrine is the most magnificently built of all birds, the most perfect flying machine. Although it nests on cliffs, in autumn the peregrine often heads for the coast where it follows the southbound shorebirds. It is one of our scarcer hawks.

Shorebirds (sandpipers and plovers) of more than a score of species swarm the mudflats in May on their way north

and again in late summer on their return. Some travel almost the length of two continents between their summer and winter homes. These long-distance travelers economize on their time by feeding when the tide is low and migrating when it is high, regardless of whether it is day or night. The yellow-legs is the self-appointed monitor of the marsh, giving the alarm with its sharp three-syllabled whistle. The dowitcher looks something like a snipe, but one would not expect to see a snipe on the open mudflats. It probes the mud with a sewing-machine motion of its long bill. The ruddy turnstone, unmistakable in its harlequin pattern, prefers pebbly beaches but it also mixes with the other shorebirds on the exposed tidal flats. The willet, a very large sandpiper, is undistinctive until it flies. Then its flashing black-and-white wing pattern identifies it.

American Eider

King Eider

White-winged Scoter

Harlequin Duck

BIRDS OF THE ROCK COAST AND THE SEA

The sea is at its best in winter. Then the countless waterbirds which breed on the fringes of the polar basin and the rocky shores of Labrador are down in our latitude, where we can see them. A headland which juts into the sea is always good—a point like Montauk at the tip of Long Island, for example. There at dawn great rafts of scoters mass off the point and fly by in smoky skeins. Most familiar is the species shown here, the white-winged scoter, or "bull white-wing" as the "coot" hunters call it. The other two scoters lack the wing patches. The surf scoter or "skunk-head" has white patches on its head; the American scoter or "butter-nose coot" is all black except for its orange bill. Gunners' names are very descriptive, but unfortunately are so local in their use that a single duck might labor under fifty or sixty names in different parts of the continent. That is why we use the standard names instead.

Although scoters nest mostly in northwestern Canada and Alaska they can be seen offshore as far south as the Carolinas or even Florida. The eiders don't travel as far. The common or American eider, the white-backed one, now nests commonly on the Maine coast, but its big flocks do not go further south in winter than Massachusetts. There, on the shoals off Monomoy, a gathering of 300,000 has been estimated. This is the same species whose down is gathered commercially in Iceland and Norway. The Canadian government has been trying to start the industry in Canada.

More northern, living close to the Arctic sea, the king eider nevertheless is the greater wanderer. Young birds are sometimes encountered on the Great Lakes or off Long Island. The brightly colored bump on the nose of the male king eider is regarded as a delicacy by the Eskimos. When they shoot one, they bite this off and chew it with great relish.

Harlequin ducks are better known on the Pacific side, but a few come each winter to the wave-washed ledges of New England. The fantastic pattern of the male makes it a rival of the wood duck in beauty.

The old-squaw, a very talkative duck, is so musical that it has been called the "duck songbird." Every sportsman who goes "coot-hunting" along the coast knows these trim little ducks with white bodies and dark wings. So deep do they dive that thousands have been taken on the Great Lakes in gill nets placed over 100 feet down.

Although one can get a taste of the rock-coast rookeries by visiting the nurseries of gulls and cormorants in Maine, one must go to the Gulf of St. Lawrence or Labrador for sheer drama. There puffins congregate in colonies of thousands of birds. With them usually are penguin-like razor-bills and murres. Gannets to the number of nearly 30,000 nest in five colonies in the Gulf of Saint Lawrence – Newfoundland area. The most famous colony, the one on Bonaventure Island, can easily be visited by boat. There the gannets are increasing; hence today we see more of them in migration, great snowy birds which wheel over the surf and plunge pelican-like into the waves.

Puffin

Gannet

Old-squaw

113

Lobster

Blue Crab

Green Turtle

Diamond-backed Terrapin

DENIZENS OF THE COAST AND THE SEA

The sea is a bountiful larder. It is unlikely that it will ever become as bare as old Mother Hubbard's cupboard. Yet, four of the creatures shown here—the lobster, green turtle, diamond-backed terrapin, and sperm whale—whose combined commercial value runs into millions of dollars per year became so diminished that regulations have become necessary. We have mined these treasures from the sea. Now we propose to treat them as a crop. *Mariculture* may yet take its place beside agriculture.

The lobster, that armor-plated crustacean with the horny boxing gloves, is bright red only after it has been dropped into boiling water. In life it is greenish, matching the sea bottom. Millions are taken each year, mostly in Maine and the Maritime Provinces, by weatherbeaten men who trap them in "lobster pots" baited with desiccated fish heads. The average lobster weighs two pounds, but giants tipping the scales at more than thirty pounds are on record. Because lobsters were growing scarcer year by year, regulations were adopted. Now no lobster under twelve inches, or some such size set by law, may be taken; in other words, no lobster that has not had a chance to free the first generation of young. Females carrying eggs are also liberated. So are extremely large lobsters over a certain size, for they are the most prolific, often laying 100,000 eggs. We now believe the lobster is here to stay.

Although the blue crab cannot match the lobster in the revenue it brings, it is worth at least half a million dollars each year. A male blue crab

Porpoise

Sperm Whale

might measure six inches across its shell. The female, smaller, lays anywhere from one to five million eggs, an incredible number. Blue crabs prefer shallow bottoms along the coast, especially near the mouths of rivers, where they skitter sidewise over the mud looking for carrion.

The green turtle, big as a tub, and often weighing 500 pounds, is called green because of its rich green fat which is made into turtle soup. Naturally, such a slow-growing animal cannot keep up with the demands of the epicures. On a June night over four centuries ago, when Ponce de Leon landed on some reefs off southern Florida he caught 160 sea turtles which had crawled ashore to lay their eggs. He called the islets the *Tortugas*, Spanish for turtles. Now, as few as four or five turtles come ashore there each season. A few of these leviathans—greens and loggerheads—still visit the coast as far north as the Carolina Capes, but soup canneries must now get them from the West Indies or the coasts of Central America.

The diamond-backed terrapin is tiny compared to the other sea turtles, with a shell only five to seven and a half inches long, yet its flesh once commanded fabulous prices. Today it is often reared in captivity, and experimental hatcheries turn out thousands. It lives in the coastal marshes and bays.

Porpoises travel in schools along our coasts, pacing the boats, leaping and playing along the bow. They are really small whales, six to twelve feet long depending on their kind. Some are known as dolphins, but this name also applies to the fish shown on page 175. Because they are small and agile porpoises have escaped the decimation of the larger whales. Whaling fleets that once sailed out of such towns as New Bedford must now use the Antarctic as their base. A recent census estimated about 100,000 whales in Antarctic waters, but it does not claim to be accurate.

Many whales strain "krill," the shrimplike creatures which swarm the ocean currents, through their comblike baleen. Whereas a loaf of bread would probably choke a whale of this type, the sperm whale shown here, the whale of the novel *Moby-Dick*, could probably have swallowed Noah. Reaching a length of sixty feet, it devours cuttlefish and even giant squids. Ambergris, the precious substance used in perfumes, is disgorged by sick sperm whales. A very sick whale once coughed up $100,000 worth.

115

Swordfish

Sergeantfish

Bluefish

Bonito

Cod

FISHES OF THE OCEAN

In the sea the turnover is terrific. It is said that only three newborn mackerel in a million survive to the tender age of three months. Even then they are only two inches long, prey to almost every larger fish that comes along—including mackerel. These larger fish are in turn pursued by still larger ones, ranging in size from the voracious bonito to huge swordfish. Enormous numbers of eggs make survival possible —or it might be argued in reverse, that survival is made possible only by eliminating most of the small fry. Otherwise the sea would not hold them all.

The swordfish (upper left) is a magnificent sight when it breaches the water in wild leaps. Lord of all game fish, it might reach a length of nearly fourteen feet and a weight of 1000 pounds (the line record is 860 pounds). Commercial fishermen out of Montauk and Block Island harpoon the basking monsters from a small "pulpit" in the bow of the boat.

Most fish vary greatly in size. Whereas a bluefish averages two pounds it might reach twenty-five. A sergeantfish averages ten but has been taken at one hundred. Nearly all of

Mackerel

Channel Bass

Pompano

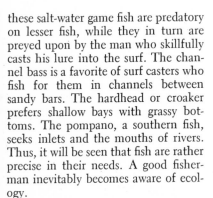

these salt-water game fish are predatory on lesser fish, while they in turn are preyed upon by the man who skillfully casts his lure into the surf. The channel bass is a favorite of surf casters who fish for them in channels between sandy bars. The hardhead or croaker prefers shallow bays with grassy bottoms. The pompano, a southern fish, seeks inlets and the mouths of rivers. Thus, it will be seen that fish are rather precise in their needs. A good fisherman inevitably becomes aware of ecology.

Perhaps the most valuable fish in the world is the cod (lower left), found in deep water on both sides of the Atlantic. In the economy of Newfoundland it is the most important source of income, bringing revenue from markets as distant as Spain and South America. Cod go about in great schools on the bottom, at depths up to fifteen hundred feet. A 50-pound cod is very large, but monsters exceed 200.

The halibut, another large bottom fish, is flattish with both its eyes on the right side like those of a flounder. A large halibut may weigh 300 or 400 pounds.

Hardhead

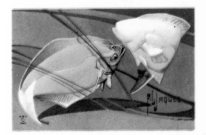

Halibut

THE SOUTH

To most northerners the South begins when they cross the Potomac River or the Ohio. But it is not all
mockingbirds and magnolias from
there on down. Actually, on the high
peaks of the Smokies, conditions are
more truly "Canadian" than they are
in southern Ontario. By simply crossing the State of North Carolina from
east to west, by climbing from the
coast to the crests, one may discover almost as varied a cross-section of American wildlife as he would by traveling
from Georgia to Maine—everything
from water-turkeys and live oaks to
crossbills and spruce trees.

The South lies within a belt where
the rainfall is from forty to fifty inches
a year, a condition magical for the
growth of green things. The extraordi-
nary variety of trees is evidence of this
fecundity. Although in this rich section of the country, one of the most
diverse on the continent, we could duplicate most of the habitats described

earlier in this book, there are also a
number of environments, which, with
their wildlife, are unique.

To some, the land below Mason and
Dixon's line means old ante-bellum
mansions surrounded by live oaks
draped with gray-green druidical
beards. Associated with these relics of
gracious living, if olfactory senses play
a part, may be the odors of jessamine
and mint julep. To others among us
the South is better symbolized by the
pines and red earth of the Piedmont.
But to insist that these are more typical
than the cabbage palmettos of the Carolina low country, the cypresses of the
Everglades, or the flaming poincianas
of Key West is to limit the South too
much. Variety is its keynote.

There is also variety in its wildlife.
Some of us think first of mockingbirds
and cardinals in old gardens with
wrought-iron gates; others of quail
flushing before the dogs on Georgia
plantations; or of egrets, pale and

ghostly, wading the cypress sloughs. No other section of our country still retains such a sense of mystery. This is particularly so in the low river swamps where few men penetrate. Behind the dark curtains of hanging moss wild turkeys can be heard gobbling at daybreak. A few bears still roam the silences and there are any quantity of the smaller fur-bearers, possums, coons, and bobcats, which venture from the shadows at night. The high country, in places, also shares with the swamps this air of the unknown.

Physically, the South may be broken into three major divisions: (1) the low country along the coasts; (2) the backbone of Appalachian Mountains; and (3) the belt of pineland, the Piedmont, separating the high country from the low. From the naturalist's point of view, the low country has the greatest lure because much of it cannot be duplicated anywhere else on the continent. This belt too can be subdivided. As we go southward along the middle Atlantic coast we notice many subtle changes. New plants and some new birds appear after we cross the mouth of the Chesapeake. Another marked change comes as we approach Charleston, South Carolina. The landscape suddenly takes on a subtropical look with squat moss-hung live oaks and plumelike cabbage palmettos. These groves, alternating with great stretches of long-leaf pines, hug the low flat country along the coast until we reach Florida, where they extend completely across the peninsula (Florida is not much more than three hundred feet above sea level at its highest point). The southern tip of Florida gives the United States its only real touch of the American Tropics. There the landscape is West Indian, with mangroves growing on stilts in the salt water, "hammocks" of West Indian hardwoods, and groves of Cuban pines (P. caribaea). Going westward from Florida the low country, or "Austral," influences rim the Gulf of Mexico and extend up the Mississippi into our heart country as far as southern Illinois, where the broad Ohio River joins the "Father of Waters." Reelfoot Lake in Tennessee is perhaps the northernmost of the true southern swamps, complete with cypress trees, water-turkeys, and water moccasins.

On the next four pages are pictured a dozen trees typical of the deep South. These are but a small fraction of the Southeast's tree flora, which numbers hundreds of species, far more than grow on the entire continent of Europe. Europe once had many more trees than it has now, but that was long before the historic period. During the glacial age the slowly advancing ice compelled trees to "migrate" southward if they were to survive. Unfortunately, Europe's main mountain ranges, the Alps, Pyrenees, and Carpathians, extending from east to west, formed a wall which blocked retreat. The hard-pressed trees survived the changing climate as long as they could and then they perished. No one knows how many species disappeared. Europe again has a green mantle of trees, but today it is made up of relatively few species. On the other hand our American mountain ranges extend from north to south. That is why our own sylva survived the glacial period. Fossils tell us that magnolias once lived in the far North. They migrated; thus today we know them as typical trees of the South.

Long-leaf Pine

Live Oak

TREES OF THE SOUTH

The flat "piney woods" of the southern coastal plain are made up of several pines—the loblolly, scrub pine, short-leaf pine, pond pine, slash pine, etc.—but none is as distinctive as the long-leaf, shown above. Rising straight as a mast, it bears great clusters of needles which measure ten to fifteen inches in length. There is no mistaking it, even from a fast-moving train. Nor can one mistake the gnarled and picturesque live oak with a spread twice that of its height. Its un-oaklike oval leaves are evergreen, festooned with beards of Spanish moss in which parula warblers tuck their nests.

The pecan, largest of the hickory clan, was once confined to the lower Mississippi Valley, but is now planted all through the South. Large thin-shelled varieties have been evolved by horticulturists. It is our only native nut tree which has been extensively developed commercially.

Holly has some commercial importance, too, especially for those farmers who sell the sprays of bright red berries and prickly leaves at Christmas time to bolster the family budget. They try to manage it carefully as a crop, yet trespassers sometimes strip the woods and carry out carloads.

Of the eight magnolias in the South (not including the exotic varieties of the garden), the handsomest is *grandiflora*, the large-flowered magnolia, with waxy white blooms eight inches across. Native to our southern coastal plain, it is now planted as far north as New Jersey. Other magnolias grow in the southern parts of the Appalachian Mountains.

Pecan

Loblolly Pine

American Holly

Magnolia

Royal Palm

Cabbage Palmetto

Saw Palmetto

White Cedar

American Corkwood   Bald Cypress

TREES OF SOUTHERN SWAMPS AND LOWLANDS

Palms symbolize the tropics. Although only a few are native, at least seventy-five species now grow in Florida. There palms from Brazil grow alongside palms from the Canary Islands, India, and South China. Of them all, our native royal palm is the most magnificent, towering one hundred feet or more on a pillar-like trunk which has the deceptive appearance of having been given a smooth coat of cement. Though planted in rows along many of Florida's fine boulevards, it may still be found wild in Everglades National Park.

The cabbage palmetto, forming islands of trees in swampy pockets, is the palm which grows farthest north, following the coastal islands north to Cape Fear, North Carolina. Its small relative the saw palmetto prefers sandier soil, often under the pines, where it never becomes more than a sprawling shrub.

In the river forests which are periodically flushed by flood waters, grows the cypress, firmly supported in the mud by spreading buttresses. Sometimes it sends up "knees" from its root system, for the purpose, some say, of "allowing the roots to breath." An ancient cypress growing in Seminole County, Florida, is believed by experts to have been there before the time of Christ.

The corkwood (above), a small scarce tree, sometimes shares the swamps with the cypress. It is very local. Another tree frequently found with the cypress is the white cedar of the Atlantic coastal plain. More often, in dark and lonely swamps, it forms dense stands of its own, so thick as to be almost impenetrable.

123

Swamp Lily

Florida Air Plant

FLOWERS OF THE SOUTH

Florida was named by the Spanish explorers for its flowers. What more inviting name could a state have? It beckons the winter visitor to a land of sunshine where the countryside is always lush and green and where flowers bloom throughout the "twelve seasons."

At the very tip of the great peninsula jutting into subtropic seas is Everglades National Park, our newest National Park and one of the most interesting. Vacationers from New York or Philadelphia who visualize an Amazonian jungle with all sorts of arboreal creatures swinging from rope-like lianas are destined to be disappointed, for only along certain creeks and in the hammocks are there trees of any size. Most of the park is made up of great expanses of sawgrass and endless thickets of mangroves. However, there is much to see. Not only is the park one of the finest natural zoos on the continent—virtually one huge aviary—but it is a botanical garden without peer.

Among the many strange flowers that greet the eye is the swamp lily (upper left), a pallid bloom which grows along rivers and in swamps from Florida to Texas. Its flowering stalk rises from one to three feet, but so edible are the frail fragrant blossoms that huge hungry grasshoppers often allow them short shrift. Some call it the spider lily, but this name more properly belongs to another group of flowers of which there are eleven in the South.

In Royal Palm Hammock at the Park ranger station you will see epiphy-

124

tic orchids leading their parasitic lives high on the spreading moss-hung limbs of some of the bigger trees. You will see air plants too, but these bromeliads, which are related to the pineapple, are even more noticeable in the cypress trees along the Tamiami Trail. They grow on the delicate branches in large dark tufts like clumps of witches'-broom or mistletoe. The air plant's stiff troughlike leaves hold water at their enlarged bases which become a catch-all for dead leaves, dust, and insects. Snails, spiders, and even small frogs live there, adding their bit to the accumulation of debris which gives nourishment to these strange plants.

One of the most striking flowers in all the South is the Texas Plume, which in spite of its name·is found eastward to Florida and north to North Carolina. Rising on a spike three or four feet tall, its inch-long trumpets invite cross-pollination by hummingbirds. It grows in patches, sometimes along the road, at other times at the edges of wood lots where the soil is sandy and sterile.

There is still much botanical exploration to be done in the South. J. K. Small's *Manual of the Southeastern Flora* lists 5557 flowering plants in the Southeast, east of the Mississippi. If we were to go west of the Mississippi into Texas, thousands of others would be added.

Speaking of Texas, we cannot omit the famous Texas bluebonnet (lower right). Proclaimed by legislative action the State flower of Texas, it is found only in south-central Texas, where it covers the fields with a carpet of blue. Many Texans confuse it with the much more widely distributed common bluebonnet.

Texas Plume

Bluebonnet

Mockingbird

Cardinal

BIRDS OF SOUTHERN GARDENS AND PLANTATIONS

Although mockingbirds turn up every year in New England and cardinals and Carolina wrens are resident as far north as southern Ontario, they are in essence true birds of the South. They are the standbys of every southern garden, as robins and chipping sparrows are in the North. Perhaps the tufted titmouse (opposite) should be included in this group of familiars.

The mockingbird, debonair and sure of itself, is like a man about town—or rather, a bird about town—arriving at the feed tray with a flip of the tail, as if to say, "Here I am." Flashing bold white patches as it flies, it can be told instantly from any other bird except the shrike, which has a black mask through its eyes. The flight of the shrike is flickering, while that of the mocker is more "like strokes of the oars of an old rowboat." Although mockingbirds sing tirelessly all day they often chant at night too, emulating the nightingale of Europe, especially on warm evenings when the moon is full. Anyone who knows the nightingale's song is struck by the basic similarity between it and the mockingbird's music—one burst of repetitious notes after another. Besides making typical "mockingbird sounds,"

the mocker does mimic other birds. The best mimics apparently are not those birds which live deep in the heart country, such as Florida and Texas. They mimic little, if at all. But those on the periphery of the range, or in localities where other mockers are not numerous, are usually excellent mimics. A good Maryland or Virginia mockingbird may imitate as many as thirty-five other species.

If a vote were taken to determine America's "favorite songster," it would probably turn out to be the mockingbird. The "best-known and best-loved" bird would unquestionably be the robin, while the title "best-looking" would no doubt go to the cardinal. We take the handsome cardinal for granted, but visitors from Europe, where there are no common bright-red birds, gasp when they see their first one. People react to red. One fellow bird artist, who has made at least twenty paintings of cardinals, tells me that no matter what kind of job he turns out, he can always sell it. A town bird, the cardinal has been increasing and spreading northward during the past forty years, ever since its caging was outlawed. Now it is among the commonest birds of such cities as Washington and Cleveland, where within the memory of living men it had been scarce.

The male painted bunting would win, hands down, the vote of "most gaudy." Its coat of many colors can be matched only by certain parrots and by a few other birds of the tropics where it spends the winter. During summer it consorts with its demure mate, a little green finch, in gardens on the outskirts of Charleston and New Orleans.

The tufted titmouse rates among the six or eight commonest woodland birds of the South. No recluse however, it also likes the live oaks near houses. Tempted by peanut hearts, sunflower seeds, or suet, it may become so tame that it will take food from one's fingers.

There are two "redbirds" in the South—the cardinal, or "winter redbird," which stays throughout the year, and the summer tanager, or "summer redbird," which returns to the tropics. Easily known from the cardinal by the fact that it has no crest, the summer tanager calls *chick-i-tuck* from the live oaks and occasionally sings its short robin-like phrases. Whereas this species rarely crosses Mason and Dixon's line, the scarlet tanager (page 60) spends its summer among Yankee woods.

Among the least of the birds familiar to every low-country plantation is the gnatcatcher, a mockingbird in miniature. It utters a thin, peevish *zpee* as it searches the Spanish moss for aphids and other tiny six-footed fare. The handsome lichen-covered nest, camouflaged to look like a knot on a limb, is rather easy to locate if you watch the bird's actions.

Painted Bunting

Tufted Titmouse

Summer Tanager

Blue-gray Gnatcatcher

127

American Egret

Wild Turkey

Mississippi Kite

Prothonotary Warbler

BIRDS OF SOUTHERN SWAMPS

A southern river swamp is a sort of never-never land. In fact some swamps are so impenetrable that they might as well be under lock and key. Anything might live in them—even ivory-billed woodpeckers (see page 15). A pair of these archaic-looking woodpeckers which are as big as ducks was recently discovered in the Appalachicola River system in northwestern Florida. However, every southern river forest has its pileated woodpeckers (page 58) which are sometimes mistaken for ivory-bills. Even the Carolina paroquet, believed extinct since 1920, is a wistful hope still entertained by some bird-watchers.

At the beginning of the century the white herons—the stately American egret (upper left) with the golden bill and the smaller snowy egret (upper right) with "golden slippers"—were almost gone. They were no longer seen flying like angels through the dark cypress sloughs. Plume scouts employed by the military trade had tracked down colony after colony and destroyed them in the name of fashion. Women wanted the filmy plumes for their silly-looking hats. They had little realization that these bridal plumes were ripped from the backs of nesting birds and that the parentless young starved to death until the whole colony was a place of death and decay. When only a few colonies remained—a few hundred birds hidden in the deepest swamps—the plume-scalping was outlawed. The first Audubon warden, Guy Bradley, was shot to death when he boarded a boat to look for illicit

128

plumes. His sacrifice and those of others saved the egrets from what seemed certain extinction. Now the American egret again nests as far north as New Jersey and Lake Erie, and the snowy egret has bred on Long Island. After the nesting season each summer there is a northward movement of the white herons (which include the immature of the little blue heron, lower right). Hundreds often reach New England and the Great Lakes. The biggest northward exodus in our memory, that of the summer of 1948, became big news in the press. In the whole history of ornithology there is no more dramatic proof that conservation is not just an idealistic dream.

Although the big waders or "glamour birds" are the most conspicuous dwellers of the river swamps, many other birds share the shadows with them. In the sepulchral aisles of the cypress the prothonotary warbler (lower left) flits like a flame, and sings its emphatic *tweet, tweet, tweet, tweet, tweet.* Where the swamps are drier, in the "second bottoms" where oak, ash, and tupelo grow, wild turkeys scratch for a living among the leafy litter. Very wary, they are a test of the skill of the woodsman who would bag one. An adaptable bird, the turkey also lives in pine woods and in the mountains.

The graceful kites, harmless hunters of snakes, lizards, and insects, have all but disappeared from many parts of the South. It is a great pity. The fact that they are related to the hawks has been held against them. Arthur Wayne, famed low-country ornithologist, once told me he used to see migrations of thousands of Mississippi kites over his home in South Carolina. "Lately," he said, "they have become almost as scarce as angel's visits."

Snowy Egret

Little Blue Heron

129

Jacana

BIRDS OF THE SUBTROPICS

Speaking of "glamour birds," southern Florida and the southernmost tip of Texas have more than their share. At these two points wanderers from the tropics often cross our borders.

White Ibis

Although we might call the white ibis tropical, it nests as far north as Fairlawn Plantation near Charleston, South Carolina. However, the biggest concentrations of these "white curlews" with red faces are in Florida and Texas. People who live in Miami or West Palm Beach sometimes see long ribbons of ibises flying over their homes on their way to nearby colonies. Colonies of one hundred thousand or more are known in Florida. Great flocks of both white ibises and wood ibises are certain to be seen by visitors to Everglades National Park. This, our newest National Park, was set aside not for its scenery but because of its unique wildlife values.

Flamingos have never been known to nest in Florida, but stray birds sometimes wander over from the Bahamas. Incidentally, the ones at Hialeah Race Track are wing-clipped captives. For many years there was an enormous colony at Andros Island in the Bahamas, but it was reported broken up during World War II. Perhaps some of the birds from Andros helped form the

Flamingo

130

Roseate Spoonbill

Reddish Egret

spectacular colony recently discovered by the Audubon Society on the coast of Yucatan.

Another showy pink bird, the roseate spoonbill, nearly disappeared from our country, but a small colony discovered on the Texas coast responded to protection until now there are thousands. The small nucleus in Florida did not show a similar response until the Everglades National Park was established. Now there is a boom in spoonbills there as well.

The reddish egret, a shaggy heron which executes an eccentric dance when catching killifish in the shallows, has also been brought back from near extinction along the Texas coast. Certain islands were set aside for them with the result that thousands now live along the Gulf coast.

The best place to see the black-bellied tree-duck and the jacana, a swamp wader with incredibly long toes, is near Brownsville, Texas. Unfortunately, the resacas, the lagoons where the old bed of the Rio Grande used to be, have been drained one by one until few remain. When the last resaca gives way to grapefruit groves, these interesting visitors from Mexico will be of little more than historical interest.

131

Black-bellied Tree-duck

Peccary

Armadillo

MAMMALS OF THE SUBTROPICS

Mammals do not recognize political boundaries. They may, from time to time, slip from Mexico across the Rio Grande into Texas, unmindful of the vigilant border patrols which are entrusted with the task of making their human brethren observe the rules. Or they may wander across the deserts into the wild border mountains of New Mexico or Arizona. The coati, not shown here, a raccoon-like animal with a slender snout and a tapering tail, has been doing this of late and seems to be increasing on our side of the line. I myself have seen little bands in the Huachuca Mountains in Arizona. Once I even saw a stray coati in the Aransas Wildlife Refuge in Texas. That same morning I saw my first peccary, the little wild pig of Mexico, so unlike the obscene porkers of the barnyard or the feral razorbacks that root about in southeastern pine woods and swamps. It was as shy as any wild thing could be, and bolted headlong for the nearest oak motte as soon as our jeep appeared. These little desert pigs often go in bands of fifteen or twenty and

are said to be dangerous if confronted, but ordinarily their first instinct is to scamper madly into the scrub. It is estimated that there are 100,000 in Texas.

Few places are as rich in mammals as the Aransas Refuge just mentioned. One of the "super refuges" operated by the U.S. Fish and Wildlife Service, it is particularly famous as the winter home of the last of the whooping cranes. At dusk on the refuge we are almost sure to see armadillos scuttling across the road. These curious armored fellows, about two feet long, not including the tail, have eight or nine movable bands or joints around the middle, which permit them to roll up in a ball, as well protected as any turtle. Sometimes in the daytime we discover one rooting the earth for insects. Its sight and hearing are so poor that we can often steal very close, particularly if we approach from behind when its head is down. However, once it discovers us, it can put on a surprising burst of speed. Although the armadillo has recently extended its range through southern Texas and Louisiana

132

to Mississippi, its sudden appearance in central and eastern Florida is a puzzle. No one is quite sure how it got there. Perhaps captive armadillos escaped.

Three tropical cats once lived along the Rio Grande. The jaguarundi cat, not shown here, barely reaches our limits. Twice the size of a house cat it has been described as looking "like a cross between a cougar and a weasel." It may be either red or gray, just as a screech owl might, and whether it is "blonde or brunette" has nothing to do with age, sex, or season. Although once a regular inhabitant of the dense thorny thickets of mesquite, catclaw, and cactus near the mouth of the Rio Grande, some authorities question whether it is still there. Certainly it is scarce.

The ocelot, a handsome spotted cat, can still be found within our borders. Twice the size of a house cat, this mild-mannered feline hides in thickets so dense that dogs can scarcely penetrate, and comes out only at night to do its hunting. So wary that it would shun the moonlight if it could, it is seldom seen even where it is common. It is furtive as a fox, and rather than depend on its own claws it lets the cruel thorns of the thickets rip up its pursuers.

The jaguar, "el tigre," is the largest of all American cats, heavier even than a cougar. Resembling the African leopard, but with a shorter tail, it may weigh 250 pounds or more. The largest ones live in Paraguay, the smallest in Mexico. Ranging hundreds of miles from the tropical forests of Mexico, jaguars were once common in southern Texas. Even in recent years one occasionally enters Texas or Arizona, giving rise to lurid Sunday supplement stories.

Jaguar

Ocelot

133

Sailfish

Yellow Grunt

FISHES OF SUBTROPIC SEAS

A diving helmet helps if you would see what goes on beneath Florida's blue coastal waters. It is like entering another world to submerge and set foot among strange coral formations where schools of brightly colored fish speed by. But so limpid is the water that even from your boat you can easily see fish eight or ten feet down. The reefs off the Florida Keys make a fascinating fishing ground where the angler can spot his fish before dropping his line down into the watery gardens of sea fans, corals, and anemones.

Next time you visit Florida, by all means stop at "Marineland," on the east coast. In this world-famous salt-water aquarium, fish, porpoises, and sea turtles live their lives together much as they do in the ocean.

The "spearfishes," which include the sailfishes, marlins, and swordfish, are the giants among salt-water game fish, inferior in size only to some of the larger sharks. Breaching the water in wild leaps, "tail-walking," and in general putting on a spectacular aerial display when hooked, they are the supreme test of the sport fisherman's skill. Both the sailfish and the blue

Blue Marlin

134

Flying Fish

Barracuda

Blue Angelfish

marlin cruise the warm waters of the Gulf Stream. Although a sailfish averages about 35 pounds and the record is 106, it looks very much larger because of the broad sail-like dorsal fin. The blue marlin is a bigger fish. The official line record is 737 pounds, but it is said that commercial fishermen off Havana, Cuba, by drifting their lines deep, have taken them up to 1500 pounds.

Flying fish, typical of the warm waters of the Gulf Stream, shoot over the waves like silvery ghost fish when the boat bears down upon them. A flying fish gliding on extended fins may travel two or three feet above the water for a distance up to one-eighth of a mile.

The wolfish-looking barracuda, recognized by its cruel teeth and the scattered black spots on its sides, is one of the few really dangerous fish. It sometimes attacks bathers. Sharks, which are relatively harmless, usually get the blame for such attacks.

Schools of yellow grunts, shown on the page opposite, live among the sea fans and corals of the Florida Keys, and so do various angel fish. The blue angel fish is one of the most beautiful.

135

GRASS COUNTRY
The Prairies and the Plains

Four centuries ago, when Castaneda came up from Mexico with Coronado, he was overwhelmed by the immensity of the Great Plains. Seas of grass extended from horizon to horizon, domed over by 180° of blue sky. He wrote, "Who would believe that 1000 horses and 500 of our cows and more than 1500 friendly Indians and servants in traveling over these plains would leave no more trace where they had passed than if nothing had been there—nothing?"

In those days the continent was primeval, the way it had been for centuries. About half of the United States was forest. Most of the other half was grass; tall grass in the moist prairies of the Mississippi basin, shorter grass in the dry country further west. Today most of the lush long-grass prairie has been put to the plow. Wheat and corn (both of which are grasses) now stretch to the horizon, and even in fields where livestock graze imported grasses replace the original native species. In fact, things have changed so completely that a few years ago, two botanists had to travel something like 30,000 miles, crossing and crisscrossing the Mississippi basin, to locate surviving specimens of certain grasses that once flourished there.

West of the 100th meridian the native grasses still dominate but they are hardly in the healthy state in which Lewis and Clark found them. Hundreds of millions of acres, forming the largest and most important grazing area in the nation, have tried to support too many cattle. The millions of buffalo were killed to make room for millions of beef cattle. Seventeen million head of livestock are pastured on our western range, which some experts say should now carry only eleven million. There was a time when twice that many could have been supported comfortably. But the practice of pasturing three or four steers where there should have been but one has deteriorated the range.

Even so, where the grass is short and rainfall light, cattle are the only safe crop (if there are not too many). When the sod is broken by the plow, wheat may be raised during wet years, but when the dry cycle swings round, the crops and landowners are ruined—and so is the soil itself. The parched earth, unprotected by a covering of turf, is whirled into the wind and piled in deep drifts. Thus the dust bowl was born in the thirties. In those dark years storms covering as much as 300,000 square miles swept up to 300,000,000 tons of powdery soil into the air. Winds blowing out of the West darkened the skies over Chicago. A film of dust even covered desks in New York City, and red snow fell in New England. A famous story tells of a Nebraska farmer sitting on his porch during a dust storm. When asked what he was doing he replied, "Watching the Kansas farms go by." It took years to restore life to this new desert which was forming in the heart of our continent.

Trees are dramatic. The public demands their conservation. But grass, being humble, has been abused and neglected.

The grasslands, a belt hundreds of miles wide, separate the green woodlands of the East from the pine-clad slopes of the Rockies. Many birds and mammals never breach this broad gap. Some follow the thin line of trees along the rivers as far as they dare, but the grass country is a barrier. Were it not for this "great divide," there would be much more homogeneity in American wildlife. East would be more like West.

On the other hand the grass country is endowed with its own rich fauna. At one time, before cattlemen took over, the Great Plains rivaled the African veldt as a home of big game. Today but a fragment of the spectacular horde remains. Buffalo were quickly reduced from herds of millions almost to zero. The last few survivors were spared just in time. Today in the United States an estimated 3700 (not counting those in Yellowstone Park) are allowed to live in scattered herds. Elk, deer, and antelope have had a similar history on the plains. This area, once by all odds the most fabulous big-game country in America, is now one of the poorest regions.

Two winged migrants of the prairies and plains—the whooping crane (page 14) and the Eskimo curlew were brought to the edge of extinction. Besides these, many others became noticeably fewer, not simply because they were overshot, but as the result of an even more potent factor. Their ancestral homes, the lakes and sloughs which dotted the northern prairies, were drained and put to the plow. This reduced the entire water-table. During dry years when even the river bottoms turned to dust, waterfowl raised few young.

The climatic conditions which brought disaster to the birds brought disaster to the homesteaders too. One after another they went broke and the land was put on the block for tax money. The Federal government, which had originally been the donor of much of this land, now bought up many sections at a very low cost, and turned some into wildlife refuges. By careful management the U.S. Fish and Wildlife Service has already done much to restore wildlife to the plains.

Sharp-tailed Grouse

Prairie Chicken

BIRDS OF THE PRAIRIES AND PLAINS

The Cree Indians must have got an idea for their dances from the sharp-tailed grouse. Watch a group of these brown chickens perform. See them pivot with rapidly stamping feet, heads down, tails up. They are perfectly synchronized. When one stops, all the dancers stop; when one shuffles his feet, all shuffle. It takes little imagination to see the prototype of a Cree dance here.

The sharp-tail is not so much a bird of the open grassy prairies as is the prairie chicken. It prefers more brushy terrain, such as the scrubby "prairie islands." A hundred years ago the prairie chicken was the number one gamebird of the midwestern grass country. It still held that rank fifty years ago, even though greatly reduced. Today the pheasant is by all odds the most numerous upland gamebird in those same States. A farm bird in China before it came here, the ring-necked pheasant fitted into our agricultural economy, while the prairie chicken did not. Today the latter bird is found only in those places where the native sod has never known the plow, or where prairies once cultivated have been retired to permanent grassland. In Missouri prairie chickens now occupy only one tenth of their ancestral range. There they follow a cycle, fluctuating between 5000 and 15,000 birds. The Conservation Commission of Missouri has done fine work studying and managing prairie chickens and so have Wisconsin and several other states, but never again will there be as many of these superb upland gamebirds as there were before the plow ripped the primeval turf. Canada, on the other hand, probably has more prairie chickens than before, because the species has pushed northward into parts of the prairie Provinces where it was unknown when the first settlers arrived.

Prairie chickens gather each spring on their dancing-grounds, where the males strut, dance, and "boom." Brilliant orange-yellow air-sacs on the sides of the neck are inflated and long neck feathers (pinnae) are erected. The "booming" of the courting males is a hollow three-syllabled *oo-loo-woo*, suggesting the sound made by blowing across the mouth of a Coca-Cola bottle.

Although the nighthawk (which is not a hawk) is found from coast to coast, nowhere is it more noticeable than on the plains. In flight the white "window" across each narrow wing is its best field mark. In courtship the male folds his wings and drops earthward like a dive-bomber, zooming up sharply with a sudden deep whir that sounds like the well-known "Bronx cheer." On the plains, where nighthawks are paler, they often sit and doze all day on rocks which are so hot that one could fry eggs on them.

The scissor-tailed flycatcher (right) is a bird of the southern plains. There it lives about ranch houses and perches on wires at the edge of town the way a kingbird might. Like the kingbirds it is a scrapper, expert in aerial tactics when a slow-moving hawk sails by. Although Texans proudly claim the scissor-tail as their own, calling it the "Texas bird of paradise," a movement was launched in Oklahoma to make it their State bird instead of the Bobwhite.

When an Easterner speaks of "cranes" he usually means herons. Cranes are strictly birds of the prairie marshes and bogs. The sandhill crane (lower right), is a long-legged, long-necked gray bird with a bald red forehead. Individuals are often washed with rusty red. Some ornithologists believe iron in the water causes this. When a crane flies its neck is fully extended; a heron makes a loop of its neck and pulls its head back to its shoulders. Large flocks of sandhill cranes still stop during migration in a few spots on the plains—along the big bend of the Platte River in Nebraska, for example—but most of these are Canadian cranes, en route to or from the prairies of Texas and Mexico. Today comparatively few cranes still nest in Wisconsin, Minnesota, or the Dakotas.

Would you believe that the "bread basket" of our continent is also one of

Scissor-tailed Flycatcher

Eastern Nighthawk

Sandhill Crane

Long-billed Curlew

Golden Plover

Hudsonian Godwit

Black-necked Stilt

the world's greatest water-bird nurseries? The myriad lakes and sloughs of the northern prairies are populated in summer by many of the same ducks that live along the seaboard in winter. Even birds which we usually think of as "sea birds"—gulls, terns, and cormorants—are numerous on certain prairie lakes.

In migration, swarms of shorebirds, using the prairies as a short cut to the Arctic, put down at the edges of the rain puddles and the ponds to feed and refresh themselves before rushing onward. A generation ago, they were considered fair game, but because of the disappearance of the Eskimo curlew and the great reduction of the long-billed curlew, golden plover, Hudsonian godwit, black-necked stilt (all shown on this page), and others, the season was closed. Shorebirds made unsatisfactory gamebirds because they could not stand up under gunning pressure. They lay but four eggs or less (ducks and grouse lay a dozen or more) and they bunch so tightly that the poorest shot can hardly miss. We read in the early records such statements as this: "Ninety-six red-backs tumbled at one discharge," and Audubon himself wrote that he witnessed 127 dowitchers killed by discharging three barrels. No wonder the shorebirds melted under the barrage like snowflakes in a summer snowstorm.

The golden plover and the Hudsonian godwit, long-distance champions among bird migrants, spend the winter on the Argentine pampas and summer on the Arctic tundra. Theirs is a clockwise migration—over the ocean from Nova Scotia to South America in the fall, back via the prairies in the spring.

The stilt (lower left), the most

140

gangly of all the shorebirds, is southern, nesting only as far north as Nebraska. The long-billed curlew once bred east to the plains of Illinois, but now you must go to the high plains of the Dakotas or to the Great Basin to find it. The U.S. Fish and Wildlife Refuges are doing much to bring back birds such as these, even though their main purpose is to act as "duck factories."

Franklin's Gull

No bird has benefited more from the federal refuge program than has the Franklin's gull. Cross the Dakotas in late summer and you will seldom be out of sight of these lovely prairie doves hawking for grasshoppers. At Sand Lake in South Dakota after they flooded the marsh, 6000 Franklin's gulls nested the first year; 60,000 nested the fifth year! In migration a single flock ten miles long and a mile wide was estimated at a million birds! Proceeding southward in swarms that look like snowflakes glinting in the sun, they journey thousands of miles to their winter rendezvous off the coast of Peru.

Snow Goose

The blue goose (identified by its white head) comes through the prairies in flights that stagger the imagination. En route from the Louisiana marshes to their summer home in Arctic Baffinland they assemble by scores of thousands in a few favored spots to rest and feed before going on. With them are always some snow geese, white with black wing-tips, but snow geese are more abundant farther west, particularly in California. Although the Canada Goose, the familiar "honker" with the black neck, is by far the most widely known and widely distributed goose, the snow goose probably exceeds it in actual numbers.

Blue Goose

141

Coyote

Badger

Pronghorn Antelope

MAMMALS OF THE
PRAIRIES AND PLAINS

Thundering hoofs once raised clouds of dust that could be seen for miles over the unsurveyed plains. What must the grasslands have been like in those days when sixty million bison, or buffalo, and forty million antelope grazed our continent! Fabulously abundant, both were hunted almost to extinction.

It seems axiomatic that we are stirred to save things only when we are about to lose them. As a biological remnant the bison is secure now, but, the problems of human survival being what they are, we can hardly expect to preserve more than the few thousand which now roam the range. The pronghorned antelope (lower left), an important game animal, less competitive with cattle than is the bison, has been allowed to increase until by latest reports there are more than 181,000 within the United States. The pronghorn is not a true antelope, as are the antelope of the Old World. Its horns do not last a lifetime like those of the Old World antelopes, but are shed each year like the antlers of the deer. The white rump-patch which flashes like a heliograph as the animal bounds away is a signal of danger to other pronghorns, just as is the powder-puff of a cotton-tail rabbit or the flag of a white-tailed deer.

Coyotes, the little sandy-colored dogs of the open country, by working in relays can occasionally run down an antelope, but ordinarily the pronghorn is too fast, leaping along at a fifty-mile-an-hour clip for short distances. Jack rabbits are the ordinary prey of many coyotes, making up a third of their

Prairie Dog

Black-footed Ferret

diet, but coyotes will not turn up their noses even at mice. When down on their luck even carrion tastes good.

Whereas its big cousin the wolf has been completely wiped out in most places, the coyote has actually prospered. In historic times it has extended its range southward into Central America, northward through a large section of Alaska, and, lately, eastward to Lake Erie. As the "brush wolf" it is even reported in New York State. In spite of certain redeeming traits, the intelligent coyote is not much loved, but like its controversial counterpart in the bird world, the crow, it will always manage to get along.

On the pastures of the plains the steer is King. Bison have had to go because each one eats more grass than a steer, and the little prairie dogs whose towns dotted the open spaces had to go too. Although it takes 250 prairie dogs to consume as much grass as one cow, there were hundreds of millions, perhaps *billions*, of prairie dogs between the Dakotas and Texas when the first prairie schooners breached the divide. The cattlemen who followed could not tolerate the "dogs." They pressed their poison campaigns until one might now ride all day without seeing a single dog town or even a sin-

gle burrow with its occupant sitting erect before it. Although reduction of these rodents was necessary, the natural enemies of prairie dogs were destroyed too. Coyotes were shot and poisoned. It is true that coyotes occasionally raid livestock, but the big lumbering badger (left center) whose only crime is to dig up the soil to get at the rodents was trapped and shot too. And so were hawks and owls. Most of the winged predators of the prairies, birds like Swainson's hawk, the rough-leg, red-tail, and others are rodent killers. Destruction of these birds doesn't make sense.

The objection to poison as a weapon of control, no matter whether it is strychnine used in predator control or DDT used on insects, is that it is not selective. It does not discriminate between the offenders and the innocent.

The black-footed ferret (upper right) has become one of the rarest of all American animals. An arch-foe of prairie dogs, it often exterminated whole "towns" before it moved on. Now, because poison campaigns have done the work instead, this handsome member of the weasel family can no longer live in the prodigal manner to which nature had adapted it, and its extinction is feared.

THE DESERT

In the Southwest the parched land is desperately thirsty. Hundreds of thousands of square miles of sandy desert, cactus country, arid plateaus, and desert mountains lie in this region of deficient rainfall. It is a land of brilliant sunshine and dramatic variety.

Why are there deserts? The answer lies in the mountains. The mountain masses, jutting up 5000 to 10,000 feet or even more, pull the scudding clouds to their peaks and wring from them their burden of moisture. The broad, flat stretches lying behind the ranges go thirsty. The sun beats down, and they become deserts.

However, when for some obscure meteorological reason the skies allow abundant rain to fall on the open desert, the barren, seemingly sterile soil is called to life. Seeds which had lain dormant in the naked sands for a year or two, or even ten, sprout, and in a matter of a fortnight or two the desert is transformed into a gaudy patchwork of blossoms. It is an unbelievable spectacle, a story of resurrection. The show does not last long, however, and as the desert pavement bakes out, the ephemeral blossoms wilt and die. Meanwhile the cycle has been completed; seeds have been formed, to lie waiting in the parched earth until another rainy season unlocks their treasure. The seeds produced are countless. Mice, kangaroo rats, pack rats, ground squirrels, and other small mammals of the desert feed on them. So do coveys of quail, which search endlessly the loose gravel. Even so, enough seeds are overlooked to transform the desert into a lovely rock garden almost overnight when the rains come.

The plants of the xeric world, where water is scarce, fall into two categories; these fragile beauties of the flash existence which make quick use of the rains and put all their effort into showy but transitory blossoms; and the long-lived plants of the devil's garden, grotesquely beautiful growths such as the cacti, yuccas, and ocotillo, which store up moisture and defend it with armor plate and daggers. To comfort-loving creatures like ourselves the desert seems an unfriendly, almost brutal place where loose cholla knuckles lie ready to jump at the touch of a shoe and sink their painful barbs into an ankle. Yet, by this same token, the small wild things find a refuge.

Except for the frail annuals that follow the rains, almost everything that grows in the desert is armed to the teeth. Desert plants do not waste energy on broad leaves which would only transmit to the air the precious moisture which has been sucked from the earth. Instead, they are sheathed in a tough moisture-proof epidermis and guarded by defiant spines, hooks, and needles. The spindly ocotillo sends out its tiny leaves only during wet spells. The palo verde puts forth a few tiny green leaves in April, but in May, when the tree explodes into a mass of showy yellow bloom, they drop off. During the rest of the year — ten months—the palo verde looks like a brushy dead thing except for the green color of its prickly twigs.

There is infinite variety in the deserts of our Southwest. No two deserts are quite alike. The Mojave in southern California is the headquarters of the weird Joshua trees which Frémont, the explorer who found them, pronounced "the most repulsive trees in the vegetable kingdom." There is beauty, even in the grotesque, thus our National Park Service has seen fit to set aside more than thirteen hundred square miles of the Mojave and Colorado Deserts as the Joshua Tree National Monument. Near Tucson, Arizona, is situated the Saguaro National Monument, nearly a hundred square miles of giant cactus or saguaro forest (see page 146). Farther to the southwest, on the international border, is Organ Pipe Cactus National Monument, an area of over five hundred square miles, where the tall ribbed organ-pipe cactus flourishes. Fortunately desert land does not cost much, so our National Park Service has been able to set aside these and other unique areas to remain as nature monuments for all time.

When you fly over the Southwest you will notice that the desert floor is a pattern of dark clusters, specks, and polka dots. Each plant keeps its distance, drawing the meager moisture from whatever radius it can hold against its competitors.

The margin of survival in the desert is slim; yet it is astonishing how many wild things have learned to live there successfully. At midday, when the high sun makes of each saguaro or yucca a sundial, the desert may seem devoid of life. But go out at daybreak or in the early morning hours before the heat of day sends the birds under cover and notice how many there are. At night, when the sands cool off, the cactus gardens are alive with small rodents. That is when the rattler does its hunting.

Naturally, the greatest activity is near water. Where the thin green line of willows and cottonwoods traces the course of a desert stream you will always find wildlife. The mesquite thickets are good too. Thrashers, doves, and a score of other birds build their nests within their twiggy fortress. Only in the great stretches of creosote bush does the desert seem lifeless.

Ocotillo

Saguaro

Wild Verbena

FLOWERS OF THE DESERT

Unlike the verbena of the garden, the wild verbena, shown above, is usually "born to blush unseen." Growing at the rocky edges of the Arizona desert it puts most of its brief energy into producing little flat-topped clusters of pink blossoms. It is but one of the many exquisite flowers which bloom when the infrequent rains call the sterile wastes to life. Edmund Jaeger in his scholarly book *Desert Wild Flowers* figures over 760 species which grow in the deserts of California alone. The deserts of Arizona and New Mexico have an even richer flora.

When the early Spanish settlers pushed up from Mexico they noticed among the grass many tulip-like flowers with three gay petals. These they named *mariposas*, the Spanish word for butterflies. Some were yellow, others white, pale lilac, and orange. Of the three dozen species none is more startling than the desert mariposa, on the opposite page. Blooming in the Mojave Desert of California and more abundantly in the desert foothills of Arizona, it touches the harsh landscape with fire in spring.

In contrast to the frail short-lived flowers are the prickly long-lived

Devilshead Cactus

Desert Mariposa

Prickly Pear Cactus

growths of the desert. The ocotillo, or flaming sword, is one of these. Its spindly stalks, ten to twenty feet long are tipped with clusters of scarlet blossoms, suggesting the flame of a blowtorch. Rocky desert hillsides are often decorated with hundreds of clumps of these willowy witch-wands.

The saguaro, or giant cactus, is the true symbol of Arizona, where law forbids its destruction. Forty or fifty feet tall, it marches in scattered ranks across the desert pavement from the gay cholla gardens to the buttressed base of the foothills. In May it holds aloft a cluster of waxy white blossoms at the tip of each arm and wears a wreath of them on its crown. Gila woodpeckers dig their nesting holes within the saguaro's protecting ribs. Later, when these holes are abandoned, elf owls, crested flycatchers, sparrow hawks, and purple martins move in.

As if to take the curse off their deformed and forbidding bodies, the cacti are crowned with the fairest of flower faces. In hue they run the gamut of the rainbow, from the lovely deep pinks of the devilshead cactus to the golden yellows of the opuntia, or prickly pear.

147

Collared Lizard

Gila Monster

Desert Bighorn Sheep

DENIZENS OF THE DRY COUNTRY AND THE DESERT

The Southwest is America's reptile stronghold. Everything from horned toads (which are really lizards) to rattlesnakes of at least ten species live there. So do our largest lizards, but in this modern day these are but puny relics of an age when dinosaurs and other huge reptiles ruled the earth.

The collared lizard, a foot long, is dappled in dusty grays and greens. It could easily escape attention when sunning itself on a rockpile if it would only sit tight, but when the traveler approaches too close for comfort it suddenly bolts in panic, zigzagging at high speed from bush to bush on its hind legs, kangaroo-fashion.

In contrast to such agility is the gait of the Gila monster (pronounced heela), our only poisonous lizard (there is another in Mexico). Fat and sluggish, and up to two feet in length, it is patterned boldly with salmon-pink and black, like some beadwork creation of a Navajo. Aroused, it can rush and snap with surprising suddenness, but must turn over on its back to inject the poison through its grooved teeth. Death to humans by Gila bite is almost unknown, Sunday supplement horror stories to the contrary notwithstanding. Like the saguaro cactus that swells during the rains and shrinks during dry spells, the Gila monster stores fat in its tail when times are good, becomes thin-tailed when starving.

The desert and the desert mountains abound in mammals too, particularly the smaller ones of the

148

chisel-toothed tribe. The black-tailed jack rabbit which can outrun almost any dog except a greyhound is found throughout the desert country and particularly in the chaparral-covered foothills. The white-tailed jack rabbit inhabits the northern plains.

The ring-tailed cat (not really a cat), a graceful, alert little animal, invites love at first sight. Haunting old pueblos, cliff dwellings, and mine tunnels at night, this shy big-eyed mouser is often called the "miner's cat." With a little encouragement it makes a confiding pet.

Ring-tailed Cat

Black-tailed Jack Rabbit

Among mammals classed as big game is the desert bighorn, one of the most magnificent sheep in the world. Once very abundant, there are now only a few remnants, an estimated five or six thousand, scattered throughout California, Nevada, Arizona, and New Mexico. A fellowship study conducted jointly by the National Audubon Society and the University of Arizona indicated that illegal killing and lack of dependable water holes were the main causes of the bighorn's depletion in Arizona. There apparently is food enough.

Water is always a problem in the desert, a problem that is becoming more acute as cities pipe it out of the mountains for their own use. When water is scanty, growth is often stunted, as it is in the little Sonora deer (lower right), a race of the white-tailed deer which does not exceed eighty pounds. In the Florida Keys there exist a few individuals of an even smaller race, the "Key deer" which weighs between forty and fifty pounds —like toys when compared to the big white-tailed bucks of the Northeast which may weigh as much as three hundred!

Sonora Deer

Scott's Oriole

Vermilion Flycatcher

Road Runner

BIRDS OF THE DESERT AND THE DESERT MOUNTAINS

No area of its size in America boasts so many kinds of songbirds during the nesting season as the southeastern corner of Arizona. In this historic land of the Apache one can climb from the scorching desert to cool fir-clad peaks in a matter of hours, passing through four or five "life zones," but the real reason southern Arizona has the edge on the rest of our southwestern desert country is that certain Mexican birds like the blue-throated hummingbird and red-faced warbler (opposite page) cross our borders there.

Scott's oriole (upper left), addicted to the desert, is seldom found far from tall yuccas. There it tucks its nest under the leaves or beneath the thatch of dead daggers. One who hears this attractive oriole for the first time usually thinks he is listening to the flutelike notes of the western meadowlark.

The vermilion flycatcher bears the appropriate scientific name *Pyrocephalus*, "firehead." Although one expects drab colors on desert creatures and particularly on flycatchers, this gaudy gem ranks as one of the most stunning of all American songbirds. Resident along our borderland from Texas to California, it is particularly conspicuous about the cottonwoods and willows that line the streams of southern Arizona. There it dances its sky dance. Mounting upward on curiously flipping wings for fifty or seventy-five feet it pours out its heart to the gray female perched demurely below.

The road runner has been described as "a cross between a chicken and a

150

Blue-throated Hummingbird   **Red-faced Warbler**

magpie." Actually it is a cuckoo that runs on the ground, a cuckoo with vastly more personality than the other rather clammy members of its tribe. Of this odd, yes queer, bird George Sutton writes, "He who really knows the road runner has risen morning after morning with the desert sun; thrilled at the brilliance of the desert stars; seen day turned to sudden night by the dust storms; pulled cactus spines from his shins." Nearly two feet long, including its flexible tail, it is an engaging clown with an expressive crest which it raises and lowers. A killer of small snakes, it offers no quarter, but seems to prefer lizards, which it chases down like a broken-field runner. Appropriately, the road runner has been nominated the State bird of New Mexico, but it might be found anywhere in the desert from Texas to California.

The blue-throated hummingbird, above, is the largest of the fourteen hummers which cross our borders. The thirteen western species are shown in full color at page 98 of *A Field Guide to Western Birds*. Flashing its iridescent gorget, the blue-throat dashes about the canyons in the mountains of southeastern Arizona and probes the scarlet monkey flowers and long-

spurred yellow columbines. Residents of the canyons of the Huachucas who attract it to their gardens with offerings of sugar water are sometimes rewarded by having it build its nest on nails projecting from their porches or outbuildings. The blue-throat can also be seen in the Chisos Mountains, in Big Bend National Park, Texas. In this new National Park American tourists can get a glimpse of Mexican wildlife without crossing the international boundary.

Of the fifty-four species of warblers which cross the Mexican border, none are more attractive than the painted redstart and the red-faced warbler, our only two warblers dressed in rose-red. The latter species is shown above. Living in the mountains of southern Arizona, way up in the pine belt, this gay mite is seen by few men except those of us to whom no tree is too tall, nor no bird too small to be scanned with our Bausch and Lombs.

A trip to the desert is an experience no American should miss during his lifetime. If birds be your goal, choose the month of May and do not restrict your activity to the low desert alone. Climb a canyon to the high country. You will be fascinated by the constant changes in the bird life.

THE WEST

A sign in Schenectady, New York, reads "The Gateway to the West." This might conform to some Bostonians' idea of the West or to that of some New York industrialists to whom anything away from the Atlantic seaboard is "West." But from the naturalist's point of view it is far from the truth. In dividing our country according to the distribution of plants, birds, and other living things most biologists draw the line at the 100th meridian. This arbitrary line passes through the central parts of the Dakotas, Nebraska, Oklahoma, and Texas. There on the plains is the great natural division, the barrier beyond which many things not adapted to the open spaces cannot pass. As you go westward beyond that invisible threshold, one eastern mammal or bird after another no longer is seen; its place is taken by some western form. Eastern birds follow the scant line of trees along the rivers as far as they can while the western birds begin to appear on the drier outcroppings. It is the area of overlap where the birdwatcher must carry both eastern and western *Field Guides*, one in each side pocket. Even so, many species of mammals and nearly half of the birds are common to both the East and the West. The ducks are almost identical, and the majority of shorebirds, terns, and hawks are the same. Songbirds differ more widely; but even many of those are transcontinental. Some of the woodland birds bridge the gap by way of the forests of Canada north of the plains. There are, in all, more species of birds and mammals between the Rockies and the Pacific than there are in the eastern three-fifths of the continent.

The reason for this rich variety lies in the physical diversity of the West. No less than 1500 peaks thrust their snowy summits 10,000 feet or more above the level of the sea. In direct contrast are the low, hot deserts, and inland "seas" such as Great Salt Lake and Salton Sea. California leads all other states in the variety of terrain. There, within sight of each other is the lowest spot in the United States, Death Valley, 280 feet below the level of the sea, and the highest, Mt. Whitney, whose bald summit climbs nearly three miles into the blue California sky. No wonder Hollywood directors boast that without leaving the state they can duplicate almost any scenery —the Sahara, the shores of the South Seas or the Mediterranean, the African veldt, the Canadian Northwoods, or the high Alps. Little wonder either, that so many of our best field biologists have come from the West. The story of ecology, the relation of the birds and mammals to their environment, is so much more obvious there; contrasts are vivid. The book of Nature is easier to read.

The West is a vertical land, of which it might be said a thousand feet of altitude equals at least two or three hundred miles of latitude. Climb a mountain canyon if you would understand the meaning of this. Take a stream in California, for example, one which comes down out of the Sierras. Start in the hot San Joaquin Valley where the stream bed wanders over the plain, and climb upward toward the distant crests.

In the valley, conditions along the streamside are not unlike those of the Carolinas or Georgia. Climbing upward, you can find the counterpart of Long Island with its oaks and pines, then Maine with its evergreen forests. If you go far enough you can almost duplicate the bleak terrain of Newfoundland or Labrador. As the plant life changes, so does the wildlife. Biologists often refer to this stratification as "life zones."

You can, therefore, change your climate almost at will. If you want snow in June, you can have it. In California, if you have had your fill of the "Floridian" atmosphere of the beaches you may, over the weekend, go skiing. You could not do that in Florida. In many parts of the West the high mountains make it possible to have a wet or dry, hot or cold climate within a few hours' reach.

You have often heard it said that the West is the best part of our great land in which to live—that in the great open spaces or even in the mushrooming towns life offers much more. Because of this reputation, several million Americans have poured into the Pacific States since World War II. This is bringing profound changes to the countryside and to wildlife. Thus, in no other section of our land is conservation more important. Because of the nature of its soils and because of its great areas of deficient rainfall, particularly in the Southwest, it cannot stand the abuse that the East has taken during the last four centuries. In a few decades, much of the West could be rendered as uninhabitable as parts of the Orient. We have had the foresight to set aside our finest National Parks, National Forests, and wildlife refuges in this spectacularly beautiful part of our continent. But there are sure to be many attacks on these institutions by selfish interests who would turn a quick dollar at the public expense. We must not let them get away with it.

Pepper Tree

Eucalyptus

TREES OF THE WEST

The Pacific coast has been planted with innumerable trees from all parts of the world. The pepper tree, above, has come to California from Peru. Eucalyptus trees, of which there are three hundred species, come from Australia. A large number of species of eucalyptus have been tried out in California, where their tall groves make excellent windbreaks and protection for bare eroded hillsides.

It is not the exotics, but the native trees, a few of which are shown on the next pages, that give the West its true character. The Monterey cypress, one of the world's most picturesque trees, is confined to Point Lobos and a two-mile stretch from Cypress Point to the shores of Carmel Bay, California. The desert palm, usually called "Washington palm" when planted in southern cities, also comes from California, where it grows wild in little oases and in certain canyons at the edge of the Colorado Desert. The home of the Utah juniper (lower right) is the Great Basin, where it is the most abundant tree.

The redwood, America's tallest tree, is known to reach a record height of 364 feet. Growing near the coast from central California to southwestern Oregon, it is exceeded in girth only by its relative the giant sequoia, or big tree, which lives in scattered groves in the Sierras. When a tree takes a thousand years to get its growth, it seems criminal for us to fell it for our transitory purposes. The Save-the-Redwoods League is campaigning to preserve as many groves as possible while there is still time.

Monterey Cypress

Redwood

Desert Palm

Utah Juniper

155

Western Yellow Pine

Sugar Pine

Douglas Fir

Colorado Blue Spruce

Eastern mountains have by far the most hardwoods (deciduous trees), western mountains the greatest variety of evergreens. First among conifers in importance is the Douglas fir (left), America's No. 1 lumber tree today. It is estimated that four hundred and fifty billion board feet of Douglas fir saw-timber still stand uncut throughout our western states. Exceeded only by the redwood and giant sequoia in size, it is the "big tree" of the Northwest. Perhaps second in importance is the western yellow pine or "ponderosa pine," whose open parklike groves and scaly reddish trunks are characteristic of the drier slopes throughout the western mountains. It might reach an age of five hundred years and a height of 230 feet, exceeded among pines only by the sugar pine, the tallest of the family. The sugar pine, confined to the mountains of California and Oregon, has the largest of all cones, measuring from a foot to a foot and a half in length—lethal missiles should they drop on one's head from 200 feet! The lodgepole pine, the most common pine of the northern Rockies, has short scrubby needles about two inches long. In dense stands the trunks grow tall and clean as masts. These slender shafts were used by the Indians for their lodges or tepees, hence the name.

Most of us know the Colorado blue spruce as the small pyramidal evergreen with silvery-blue foliage which decorates our lawns and gardens. Its real home is the Rocky Mountains, where it grows in scattered groves. There it may exceed a hundred feet in height and reach an age of 400 years. The Oregon yew, nowhere abundant, grows along the banks of mountain streams throughout the Northwest.

Lodgepole Pine

Oregon Yew

157

Scarlet Globemallow

Forget-me-not

Pride of California

Mountain Harebell

WILDFLOWERS OF THE WEST

At least 32,000 species of flowering plants grow north of the Mexican border. Here again the West seems to possess more than its share. Unique species are often known from a single valley or a single mountain range. The average person will have to feel satisfied if he merely recognizes the families to which most of them belong. Whether he can name them or not, they make exquisite subjects for his color camera.

The scarlet globemallow (upper left) that colors the Southwest with its glowing display is one of many kinds of mallows. Mallows remind us of miniature hollyhocks, which in a sense they are.

Forget-me-nots are the bluest of all blue flowers. Exquisite dwarf forget-me-nots crowd in tiny clusters in the alpine gardens on some of our highest peaks. The mountain forget-me-not, shown here, is common in the Sierras.

The harebell, above, seems almost too fragile for its rugged environment. In the Rockies it often anchors itself in the smallest of fissures and cracks.

Pride of California, the most spectacular of all the pea family, with flowers two inches long, thrives near San Diego.

Colorado Columbine

Bitter-root

California Poppy

On this page are three State flowers. The blue, or Rocky Mountain, columbine has been chosen by Colorado. Although it blooms from Montana to Mexico, nowhere does it seem as large and beautiful as it does along the lower trails leading to the peaks of the "Centennial State."

Bitter-root is Montana's State flower. Inseparable from the history of the "Treasure State," it was first noted by the Lewis and Clark expedition and was later given the generic name *Lewisia* in honor of Meriwether Lewis, who brought back the specimens. The Bitter Root Mountains and the Bitter Root Valley in turn took their names from this attractive flower which has become a symbol of Montana.

The California poppy, State flower of California has won favor in the face of stiff competition in a commonwealth noted for its gaudy flowers. Early Spanish explorers, seeing whole hillsides aflame with poppies, named the California coast the "Land of Fire." Although the great natural flower gardens along the Pacific are almost a thing of the past, we can still visualize their pristine loveliness when we visit Point Lobos where a sample has been preserved.

California Sea-lion

Spotted Skunk

MAMMALS OF THE WEST

At the Cliff House in San Francisco we can always see sea-lions. There, on the wave-washed rocks just offshore, are sometimes hundreds of them. These, we are told, are northern or Steller's sea-lions. The big ones, which are bulls, may weigh as much as a ton. California sea-lions are much smaller, males averaging about 500 pounds. The California sea-lion, incidentally, is the "trained seal" of the circus, the one taught to toot horns and bounce big rubber balls. It ranges farther south along the California coast and along the west coast of Mexico.

Unless you wish to see seals and other maritime species, by all odds the best places to go to find mammals are the National Parks and Monuments. There, where shy creatures are given full protection, they are not only more numerous but many have lost their fear. Ground squirrels beg tourists for peanuts; even a few of the deer and bears become panhandlers. The Park administration disapproves of this, however, maintaining that wild animals should remain wild. Furthermore, it isn't always safe to feed deer or bears.

Most mammals are semi-nocturnal; they avoid the noonday sun. So, if you would observe them, go forth at daybreak when it is barely light and spend the first two or three morning hours on the trails, or else, go out late in the day when the shadows begin to lengthen. The best book to slip into your pocket is the new *Field Guide to the Mammals*, by Burt and Grossenheider, in which nearly every North American mammal is shown exquisitely in full color with their "field marks" indicated.

The little spotted skunk (above), half the size of a cat, can sometimes be seen at dusk, pattering over some rocky outcropping in its lively search for insects and mice. It is a better mouser than any cat. Partial to brushy places, canyons, and deserts, it ranges from Idaho to Central America. This is the animal that the fur trade in their price lists calls the "civet cat," but it is neither a cat nor related to the civets of the Old World.

The tassel-eared squirrel, most beautiful of all squirrels, has developed two races in the Southwest. The Abert squirrel, *white* below, lives south and east of the Grand Canyon; the Kaibab

160

squirrel, black below, is confined to the Kaibab Plateau on the north rim of the Canyon. They are separated by only fifteen miles—but it might as well be a thousand. The thing they have in common is a liking for tall yellow pines.

The golden-mantled ground squirrel looks like a big chipmunk, but it is twice the size of that little animal and may be known by the bright "mantle" thrown loosely over its shoulders. Although it can climb trees, it is a true ground squirrel, inhabiting the open mountain forests where the sunlight reaches the rocks and the brown earth. Found in most western National Parks, it is such an engaging little beggar as it sits on its haunches and asks for peanuts that it often steals the show from some of Nature's grandest spectacles.

Less often seen by the park visitor is the pika, the little "rock rabbit" that inhabits the rock slides at high elevations. The mountain climber picking his way over the jumbled boulders is startled by a short, shrill bleat as one pika after another which had been immobile and invisible darts from its perch into the shadows. Pikas are haymakers, cutting grass from the alpine meadows and curing it in little stacks which might sometimes almost fill a bushel basket. Another mountaineer, the hoary marmot, a big grizzled woodchuck, lives close to timberline in our northernmost Parks, Glacier, Olympic, and Rainier. It has a penetrating whistle that can be heard a mile away. Unlike the little pika, which bravely ignores the blasts of winter, the marmot sleeps most of its life away. It may spend eight or nine months of the year in deathlike hibernation.

Kaibab Squirrel

Golden-mantled Ground Squirrel

Pika

Hoary Marmot

161

Mule Deer

Black-tailed Deer

Elk

Deer are getting along finely. While other big mammals, such as the bison and grizzly, have been almost wiped off the map, and elk, moose, antelope, and mountain sheep have been pushed back into pockets, deer have held their own. In fact, in some states there are more deer today than there were when the red man stalked them.

There are reasons for this. Anything that interfered with livestock had to go. Bison and other hoofed beasts that grazed the coveted grass had to make room for white-faced steers. Nor could the grizzly or the wolf be tolerated in the cattleman's eyes. Deer on the other hand are browsers. They eat leaves in preference to grass. As every wildlife management expert knows, there is more browse in a cut-over woodland than there is in the pristine wilderness. It has been proved that leaves touched by the sun are far higher in nutriment than those grown in the forest shade. Little wonder, then, that the cut-over forests and slashings of Pennsylvania, Michigan, and Wisconsin harbor so many hundreds of thousands of white-tailed deer today. In some places the population has built up so high that many deer starve to death in winter. We could well afford to have a few cougars, or mountain lions (upper right), to take off the weak or the sick. But today only a remnant of these big cats have been allowed to roam. They can still be found, at least occasionally, in most of our western National Parks.

Throughout the West the most widespread deer is the mule deer, estimated today at over 1,500,000. Its big muley ears and black-tipped tail are its field marks. In the humid forests along the Pacific slope the black-tailed deer (a

162

subspecies) replaces the typical form. There are more than 400,000 in the three Pacific states. The black-tail's tail, entirely black above and white beneath, is waved like a flag of truce when the animal bounds away.

A bull elk, large as a saddle horse and crowned with a rack of antlers four feet high, is a magnificent beast. Polygamous, he might claim two or three dozen wives for his harem. The treks which elk once made from their summer homes in the mountains to the valleys where they spend the winter have been hampered in recent times by the fact that the range no longer belongs to them. The rich valleys have been fenced and turned over to livestock and the plow. Thousands of elk, deprived of winter range, die of starvation some years. To alleviate a local condition the U.S. Fish and Wildlife Service maintains its famous Elk Refuge at Jackson Hole, Wyoming.

It is believed that elk at one time may have numbered 10,000,000. Now there are less than 200,000 in the United States. The pronghorn antelope (see also page 142), once estimated at 40,000,000, was recently pegged at 181,000. The Rocky Mountain sheep, or "bighorn," which once enjoyed a large population, is now down to less than 9000 which still range the western rimrock.

Of all the big mammals, the one which seems to have been least affected by civilization is the mountain goat, which roams the edges of the high snowfields in its long underwear. No one wants its bleak rocky home. Now estimated at nearly 13,000 in the Northwest south of the Canadian border, there probably never were many more.

Cougar

Rocky Mountain Sheep

Mountain Goat

Pronghorn Antelope

Varied Thrush   Western Robin

BIRDS OF THE WEST

The traveler from the East, crossing the mountains for the first time, is surprised to find that half the birds he sees in the Pacific States are birds he already knows. Of the 530 species covered in his copy of A Field Guide to Western Birds, 300 are included in his eastern book. The mourning doves look the same; so do the nighthawks, song sparrows, and red-wings, even though they are slightly different subspecies. Others like the meadowlarks, bluebirds, and flickers appear much the same too, although ornithologists regard them as distinct species. In the Northwest the birds remind one most of the birds back East. You would expect this, because there many of the woodlands and farms are not unlike those in New England. In the arid Southwest the contrast is much greater. Except along the low streams most of the birds of the dry country and the desert cannot be duplicated in the humid Southeast.

From coast to coast the best-known bird is unquestionably the robin, but its conversion to civilization is not so complete in the West. In the East most robins ignore the woods, nesting instead about the towns and farms. Although they are dooryard birds in parts

of the West too, they seem more at home in the mountain forests. There in the parklike groves of yellow pines and other conifers they build their mud-walled nests. But during the last thirty or forty years nesting robins have been pioneering more and more into irrigated country, even into the valleys of California where once they were known only as winter visitors. The important requirement for a homesteading robin is to have soil soft enough in which to dig worms and moist enough to use as mortar for its nest.

The varied thrush, upper left, is the robin of the northwestern rain forest. At close of day on the slopes of Rainier its eery harmonic whistle is a familiar sound, a long quavering note, succeeded after a pause by one on a lower or higher pitch. No other bird voice sounds remotely like it. The singer, if it can be seen in the shadows, looks like a robin with an orange stripe over its eye, orange wing-bars and a black band across its rusty breast.

The western bluebird differs from the eastern bluebird in having a blue throat and a rusty back. It summers throughout most of the West in the oak-covered foothills and in the yellow-pine belt, wherever gnarled trees offer good nesting holes. Scattering widely in winter, it is a familiar sight along country roads, easily identified by its round-shouldered silhouette as it perches on the telegraph wires and fence posts (see mountain bluebird on page 166).

Bullock's oriole (right) flashes like a flame through the trees that cluster about the ranch houses. Its accented piping notes are a characteristic summer sound in the cottonwoods and sycamores along the stream courses. Although there are four other orioles in the Southwest, Bullock's, ranging north to Canada, is the only one familiar to most Westerners. It is the western counterpart of the Baltimore oriole which lives in the elms of eastern towns. In fact, in Oklahoma where the two meet they sometimes hybridize.

The presence of water, whether it be a river, slough, or irrigation ditch, always means a concentration of birds. Nowhere is there more activity than in a tule, or cattail, marsh. Besides the grunting and gabbling of coots, grebes, and other waterfowl there are many other sounds such as the voices of yellowthroats, marsh wrens, and redwings. Most spectacular in appearance (but unlovely in voice) are the yellow-headed blackbirds which scrape out their low rasping notes "like rusty hinges on the old barn door." In migration, yellow-heads travel with the other blackbirds—red-wings, cowbirds, and Brewer's blackbirds — sweeping across the plowed fields and the stubble by hundreds and visiting the cattle tanks and corrals. The yellow-head has no counterpart on the Atlantic seaboard.

Western Bluebird

Bullock's Oriole

Yellow-headed Blackbird

Golden Eagle

Magpie

BIRDS OF THE
WESTERN MOUNTAINS

The West, as we commented earlier, is a vertical land. Four or five "life zones" might be represented on a single mountain range—*Upper Sonoran, Transition, Canadian, Hudsonian, Arctic-alpine*—to use the terms of the field biologist. Although to many birds, zones do not seem important, some are restricted to a single zone. It is a sermon in ecology to climb one of the western ranges and to see how the bird life changes with the altitude.

In the East, a little ruby-crowned kinglet (shown on page 72) might nest in New Brunswick and spend the winter in Georgia, nearly 1500 miles away. To accomplish the same thing a ruby-crown in California or Arizona might merely nest in the firs 7000 or 8000 feet up in the mountains and fly a few thousand feet down and a few miles away when winter approaches. We call this "vertical" or altitudinal" migration.

Lord of all the birds that live in the highlands is the golden eagle (upper left). It is the eagle of the mountains, whereas the bald eagle is the eagle of the big rivers and the coast. How many golden eagles there are in the West is anyone's guess. Fortunately, the rugged terrain in which they locate their eyries —the maze of canyons, cliffs, and peaks that make up the western Cordillera— discourage most egg-collectors. Were it not for those men who hunt them down by helicopter (as in western Texas) the future of their race would seem more secure than that of the tree-nesting bald eagle. The golden eagle still survives in

Mountain Bluebird

166

the British Isles whereas the sea eagle (the bald eagle's counterpart) is gone.

Magpies are cousins of the crows, but far more good-looking. There can be no mistaking them as they fly across the fields with their long iridescent tails streaming straight behind. They are birds of the sagebrush country, valley ranches, and foothills in the cool, rather dry sections of the West. You will not see them on the Pacific slope.

The mountain bluebird is like a touch of sky—pure turquoise rather than the deep violet-blue of the western bluebird (page 165). It nests in the scattered groves of the high mountains, at higher altitudes than the other bird. Both species visit the lowlands in winter.

In winter, cities like Denver, Seattle, and Portland are sometimes invaded by evening grosbeaks. The roving flocks descend on the maples and box-elders which line the streets. These chunky golden finches leave their homes in the mountain forests probably when the food supply fails. Such birds which arrive in hordes one winter, then are absent for several, we call *irruptive* or *irregular migrants.*

Steller's jay, the big dark jay with the topknot, flashes like a woodland spirit among the yellow pines on the mountain slopes and through the cathedral aisles of the coastal forests. It prefers evergreens, whereas the other widespread western jay, the scrub (or California) jay, the one without a crest, prefers oaks.

The western tanager probably merits the title of the West's "most colorful" bird. Like Steller's jay, it favors the open yellow-pine groves of the mountains, but you will often find it in the oaks too.

Evening Grosbeak

Steller's Jay

Western Tanager

White-fronted Goose

Cinnamon Teal

WATER BIRDS
OF THE WEST

A pond or bay in the Pacific States has much in common with the ponds and bays of the Atlantic seaboard. The majority of water birds that dive or dabble in them are the same. There are, however, a few waterfowl that are distinctly western, birds which we would not ordinarily expect to see in the East. Several are shown here.

The white-fronted goose which nests in Alaska flocks by thousands into the wide California valleys to spend the winter. There it consorts with hordes of snow geese, cackling geese, and Canadas to form one of the great waterfowl spectacles of the continent.

The cinnamon teal is the only dabbling duck strictly confined to the West (it replaces the blue-winged teal there). The male is deep chestnut.

Barrow's golden-eye, lower right, can be found occasionally along the New England coast, but it is more typical of the northern Rocky Mountain region, where females can often be seen on beaver ponds with their broods. The crescent-shaped face-patch distinguishes the male.

Also typical of western lakes are: the avocet, a handsome big shorebird with an upturned bill which it swings scythelike through the mud; the western grebe, our largest American grebe, which was once slaughtered for hat trimmings; and the white pelican, with nine-foot wingspread (second in the West only to the condor). Famous pelican colonies exist on Salton Sea (California), Klamath Lake (Oregon), Pyramid Lake (Nevada), Great Salt Lake, and Yellowstone Lake.

Barrow's Golden-eye

White Pelican

Avocet

Western Grebe

California Quail

Valley Quail

Gambel's Quail

UPLAND GAMEBIRDS OF THE WEST

Every last one of the chicken-like scratchers—"the upland gamebirds"—of North America can be found somewhere within the western states or in western Canada. On the other hand, none of those shown on these two pages lives in the East.

The California quail (upper left), running on twinkling legs for the nearest cover, gives the impression of a plump little chicken-like bird with a short plume that bobs over its bill. Chosen as California's State bird, it is as much at home in the gardens at the edge of town as it is in the brushy valleys and chaparral-covered foothills. Originally native to California and Oregon, it has now been transplanted widely elsewhere in the West. The bird called the valley quail is really just a subspecies of the California quail. It is the form found in the southern half of California and northward through the interior of the state.

Gambel's quail replaces the California quail in the deserts of the Southwest. It looks much the same as the California quail except for the black patch on its belly.

Ptarmigan are the little arctic-alpine

White-tailed Ptarmigan

Mearns's Quail

Sage Hen

Sooty Grouse

chickens that change their brown summer coats to white ones for winter wear. On such peaks as Rainier and the high summits of the Rockies is found the white-tailed ptarmigan. The other two ptarmigan, the rock and the willow, live in the Arctic.

Mearns's quail, the most bizarre of all the quail lives on the scrubby slopes of desert mountains along the Mexican border. The scaled quail, or "blue quail," also of the Southwest, is found somewhat more widely but is declining in numbers because its grassy haunts have been overgrazed.

The sage hen, the big grouse of the open sagebrush plains is as large as a small turkey. Scores of cocks strut and dance in a fantastic courtship in which the dominant male or "flockmaster" mates with most of the hens.

The sooty grouse lives in the shadows of the fir forests high in the mountains of the Pacific States. Lower down, on the brushy slopes of some of these same mountains lives the shy mountain quail (lower right). It takes a bit of stalking to get a good look at one, but when seen well there is no mistaking it with its long erect plume.

Mountain Quail

Rainbow Trout

Cutthroat Trout

Steelhead Trout

FISHES OF
WESTERN STREAMS

Worshipers at the shrine of Izaak Walton are aware that there is a connection between good forestry and good fishing. In our National Forests and in other well-managed timber tracts the streams run crystal clear and there is a good flow of water throughout the year, a paradise for trout.

The grayling, shown on the page opposite, disappeared from Michigan when the great forests were logged off and the streams turned too warm and silty. Although there is even a town in Michigan named Grayling, one must now go to Montana or Alaska to find this attractive fish.

The West is the headquarters for trout. The rainbow trout, upper left, originally found only in streams of the Pacific slope, has now been transplanted in trout waters throughout much of the world. Some populations of rainbows migrate to the sea. These, blue-gray in salt water, are known as steelhead trout. Upon returning they soon become almost indistinguishable from non-migratory rainbows.

The cutthroat trout, known by the red slashes on its throat, is native to the Rocky Mountain area. The beautiful golden trout, first found in Volcano Creek at the foot of Mt. Whitney, has now been planted widely in the Sierra. The silver trout lurks in the deep waters of Lake Tahoe in eastern California. The Dolly Varden trout, found in the same waters as the cutthroat and the rainbow, was apparently named by an imaginative fisherman to whom its colors suggested the dress worn by a character in one of Dickens's novels.

172

Dolly Varden Trout

Silver Trout

Grayling

Golden Trout

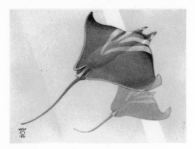

Pacific Manta

Tiger Shark

Chinook Salmon

Tuna

FISHES OF
THE PACIFIC OCEAN

The world's largest ocean is the home of some of the world's largest fishes.

The manta (upper left), "devilfish," or "sea bat," call it what you will, might measure twenty feet across and weigh 3000 pounds or more. Feared by pearl-divers and by some sailors who believe the legend that it "can seize the anchor and run away with the boat," it is really quite harmless, feeding on crustaceans and small surface fishes. Yet, it must not have many enemies, for it bears only one large young at a time, alive. By contrast, other fish are vastly prolific; some lay eggs by the million. They are forced to do so if they would survive, for in the sea, far more than on the land, nature is "red in tooth." Existence is a continuous savage pursuit to determine who eats whom.

Flying-fish flee before the dolphins or tuna that pursue them. These voracious fish, in turn, must avoid the tiger shark, a giant fifteen to thirty feet long. Its curved teeth, serrated on the margin like a patent breadknife, are ready to slash even at sharks of other species. In their stomachs are often found chunks, several pounds in weight, torn from the flanks of their relatives. Although most sharks will not attack men, tiger sharks are known to do so.

The tuna, whose rolling schools roam the high seas in their relentless pursuit of sardines, mackerel, and flying-fish, reaches a length of twelve feet or more and a weight of 1500 pounds. Superbly streamlined, this model of perfect submarine design

174

can easily keep abreast of a boat traveling at eight knots. One of the world's most valuable fish, 675,000,000 pounds are harvested annually.

The dolphin, living mostly in tropical and subtropical oceans, attains a length of six feet. The record fish caught by Zane Grey at Tahiti weighed 63 pounds. Sports fishermen comment that the brilliant hues are so evanescent that they fade before their eyes as the fish gasps its last. Porpoises (page 115) of some species are also called dolphins.

The striped bass (lower right), once found only on the Atlantic side, was shipped west as early as 1879. The 435 yearlings dumped into San Francisco Bay flourished beyond belief until, twenty years later, a million pounds a year were harvested by California fisheries. Striped bass are equally important to sports fishermen who take their gear down to the inlets and beaches on fine summer weekends.

You would think the ocean would be large enough for any fish to complete its cycle of life, yet when the time comes a salmon returns to the same river where it was born. It fights its way up the rapids and leaps the waterfalls until it reaches the headwaters, sometimes a thousand miles from the sea. There it lays its eggs before its life ebbs away. The fingerlings find their way back to the sea alone. The chinook, largest of the five Pacific salmon, gets its name from the warm southerly wind that tells the coast Indians that the ice will soon go out and that the fish will be running. Power dams like Bonneville in the Columbia have threatened the multimillion-dollar salmon industry. Fish ladders have been devised to help the salmon over these dams.

Dolphin

Striped Bass

175

THE FAR NORTH AND THE ARCTIC

The air age has opened up the Arctic. Look at a globe (not a flat map projection) and you will see that the Arctic Ocean which separates the New World from the Old is, in a sense, just a large "Mediterranean," only a fraction as large as the Pacific Ocean (one twelfth) or the Atlantic (one sixth).

The classical view was that nothing lived in the "Frigid Zone," that it was too cold, but now we know that even in the vicinity of the pole itself, crustaceans abound in the cold waters and, if there are open leads in the pack ice, seals are on hand to gulp these small creatures down. The great polar explorer Stefansson uses the phrase "the friendly Arctic," because there is actually a great abundance of life in parts of the far North, particularly during the brief summer period.

Most of us despair of ever seeing at first hand the cold lands on the roof of the world. We must be satisfied to visit the lonely hyperborean realm vicariously through color films brought back by expeditions, or through the pages of the *National Geographic*. However, Churchill on Hudson Bay, a favorite mecca of ornithologists these days, can be reached by train from Winnipeg. This outpost is perhaps the most easily accessible spot to Americans or Canadians who would get a glimpse of the Arctic.

Almost endless evergreen forests stretch across Canada. Beyond this wide belt, where the last few stunted trees give way to the barren grounds and the tundra, the Arctic begins. There the frozen ground thaws only at the surface for a few brief weeks in summer. Beneath, only a few inches down, is the eternal ice. Typical prairie-like tundra, the kind that covers most of the Canadian Arctic is dotted with innumerable ponds and lakes, which often occupy half its surface. The lakes are shallow (you can wade most of them), and many have no real outlets but are connected with each other by a honeycomb of narrow channels. Countless mosquitoes rise in smoky clouds from the edges of the glassy pools and we thank heaven for the insect-repelling "jungle oils" which the army has recently developed. "High tundra" on the mountains has better drainage; so naturally there are not so many lakes, nor so many birds either.

North of the Arctic Circle, as everyone knows, the sun never sets during a brief period in midsummer. Slowly circling around the sky, it dips low late in the evening and rises again before it touches the horizon. Round and round it goes. One needs sleep, however, even in the land of everlasting daylight, but apparently less of it. The same seems true of the birds. In Swedish Lapland I found that the birch woods and the bogs were as silent as the tomb in the early hours of the evening, even though the sun shone down, but along toward midnight one bird after another burst into song, until by 1 A.M. the chorus was in full swing. The long working day makes it possible for birds to raise a brood quickly during the brief Arctic summer. This is important because they do not have much time to spare. One ornithologist noticed that robins in Alaska worked about twenty hours a day feeding their broods. In eight and a half days the well-fledged young were ready to leave the nest. At Columbus, Ohio, where nights are long it takes a pair of robins nearly fourteen days to bring their young to the same stage.

Although many people think of the Arctic as one vast icy zone, monotonous in its sameness, it really has great variety. There are showy carpets of wildflowers, barren mountains where rock ptarmigan play hide and seek among the boulders, lake-studded prairies, drifting packs of sea ice constantly on the move, icebergs, great archipelagos, and rugged shorelines cut by deep fiords and bays. The climate of the North also varies. In Newfoundland, where the warm moist air from the Gulf Stream meets the chill breezes blowing off the icy Labrador Current, fogs and mists blot out the sun much of the time and rainfall, in places, exceeds sixty inches a year. Five thousand miles away in the Aleutian chain which fences out the warm Japanese Current it is even wetter. Two hundred and fifty rainy days during the year create an annual precipitation of eighty inches. Yet in many places in the Arctic the precipitation is scarcely six or eight inches a year, about as much as some deserts get. But the terrain is not like that of the desert. On the contrary, it is wet and boggy. Water does not sink in but lies in pools on the surface; evaporation is slow.

The tundra in summer is colorful. Tiny rhododendrons a few inches high, poppies, buttercups, saxifrages, and many other flowers spread their blooms like scatter rugs. Small butterflies of a number of species visit them. Life is vibrant, whether it is in Arctic Canada, Alaska, Iceland, or Siberia. Only Greenland with its ice-cap thousands of feet thick and hundreds of thousands of square miles in extent presents the picture of sterile grandeur which most people have in mind when they think of the Arctic.

MAMMALS OF ALASKA

Alaska is magnificent. Its mountain ranges, the highest on the continent, its far-flung tundras, lakes, dark forests, and wild coasts make a dramatic background for many big mammals. Mount McKinley National Park, our most remote National Park, harbors wolves, grizzlies, and mountain sheep, while the Aleutians and the Pribilofs know the marine mammals.

The fin-footed ones, the seals, abound throughout the northern seas, for cold water has more planktonic life in its shadowy depths than warm water, hence more fish for seals to feed upon. Of all the seals none has a story to compare with that of the Alaska fur seal. The females are great travelers, swimming south each winter to California, sometimes even to Baja California. The old bulls take no chances; they stay up in the Gulf of Alaska and get back to their rookeries in the Pribilofs as soon as they can. There, under the smoky skies of Bering Sea, the first ones back get the best ledges. Later come the young bulls. They try to get space but are usually forced to take bachelors' quarters. When the cows finally return from their long vacation, the fighting between bulls is constant. Some tough old bulls gather harems of as many as one hundred cows. During all this time, a period of three months, they are much too busy to eat.

Because their fur is so prized, the seals of the Pribilofs were slaughtered by the million, until in 1911 there remained only 124,000. It looked as though the end were not far away. But through treaties and regulations the declining herds have now been built

Fur Seal

Kodiak Bear

178

back to 3,000,000 animals. Today only young bachelor seals, three years old, are harvested. More than a million of these have yielded their coveted coats.

Largest of the world's carnivores is the Kodiak bear, which lives on Kodiak Island and along the southeastern coast of Alaska. Enormous, it might weigh anywhere from 1200 to 1600 pounds and can wave its paws twelve feet in the air when it stands on its massive hind legs. It may look clumsy, but the way it can snag a salmon from a pool with no fishing tackle but its claws is the envy of every angler. Whereas the closely related grizzly bears will eat almost anything if they can catch it, from a tiny ground squirrel to a bull elk, the big Kodiak bear seems to prefer fish to all else. Grizzlies are nearly gone in the United States, except for a few in the National Parks and Forests. A number of local forms are extinct. In Alaska there is still a good population of these goliaths.

Of all the hoofed animals, caribou are the most characteristic of the far North. They are of two main sorts, the woodland caribou and the barren-ground caribou (page 181). Stone's caribou, which lives throughout much of Alaska, is one of the barren-ground subspecies. During summer it climbs the mountains, where it pastures on the lichens and the fresh new growths that carpet the alpine meadows above timberline.

The Dall sheep or white mountain sheep, which picks its surefooted way over windswept Alaskan crags, has a white snowsuit to render it invisible against the snow fields. It is smaller and more lightly built than the Rocky Mountain bighorn, with horns that do not curl quite as tightly.

Stone's Caribou

Dall Sheep

179

Arctic Fox

Polar Bear

MAMMALS OF THE ARCTIC

The lemming is the key animal in the economy of the Arctic. There are a number of varieties of these Arctic mice, but they fall into two groups; the brown lemmings *(Lemmus)* and the collared lemmings *(Dicrostonyx)*, shown on the opposite page. The collared lemming is the only mouse that changes into a white winter suit.

Lemmings are eaten by Arctic foxes, wolves, weasels, snowy owls, rough-legged hawks, and jaegers. Even the ungainly caribou, a vegetarian, sometimes chomps them up with its big flat teeth. Yet with such a host of enemies the lemming outbreeds them. With five or six young in a litter, and five or six litters a season—perhaps more—lemmings are soon out of hand, eating themselves bankrupt. Then comes the crash. It usually takes place every fourth year (sometimes third or fifth). They die of starvation and disease. Some brown lemmings apparently indulge in the senseless migrations to destruction which lemmings are so famous for, but not so spectacularly as the Norwegian lemmings, which swarm across every obstacle — rocks, ponds, even fiords and arms of the sea. When the crash comes in the

American Arctic, the snowy owls, hungry, move south across the Canadian border in thousands. Most of them meet death by shotgun fire. Very few return. The white foxes travel, too, and many starve to death. The poor Eskimo, in turn, has a bad year. No furs mean no supplies at the Hudson's Bay Post, unless he can get credit.

The Arctic fox, which turns white in winter, is quite an adaptable creature, though. It often wanders far offshore on the pressure ice, gleaning gifts cast up by the sea. If a polar bear makes its headquarters on the floe, the little fox is in luck, for the main food of the big white bears is seals. After a kill, the foxes, like jackals, wait for the leavings. If a whale is stranded, a hundred foxes can live off the carcass.

Musk oxen, the shaggy cattle of the Arctic, have grown scarce. Wolves are not a great problem to them because the little herds do not flee like caribou but stand their ground, forming a phalanx—an almost impregnable circle. If a wolf threatens, a pair of horns is always ready to toss it aside. However, when the Eskimos first received firearms, they began an orgy of killing. The ancient circle formation no long-

Collared Lemming

Musk Ox

er had to be respected. Each animal could be picked off one by one, until none remained. In 1934 it was estimated 13,000 musk oxen were left in Canada, most of them on the remote Arctic islands.

Whereas the woodland caribou of the Canadian forest has grown much scarcer, the barren-ground caribou still exists in places in large numbers. Stefansson believes a possible estimate for Canada would be five million. Other authorities consider this figure far too high. Caribou are able to survive in the northern parts of the northernmost islands in the world. Because they love reindeer moss, and because these big gray lichens take years to grow, herds of caribou must keep moving. They seem always to be on the go, crossing streams, heading for the horizon in straggling bands. Migrations of a million caribou have been described.

The reindeer is a domesticated Old World form of the caribou. Twelve hundred reindeer, introduced into Alaska over fifty years ago to assure a stable food supply for the Eskimos, increased to more than one million head, but now have declined badly because of poor management.

Barren-ground Caribou

BIRDS OF THE ARCTIC

The far North, with its myriad unnamed lakes, is the great nursery of millions of waders and other aquatic birds. Spring comes explosively, and the relatively birdless tundra, still thawing, becomes populated by shorebirds almost overnight. Pairs are scattered far and wide over the swales, courting, carrying on, and getting ready to nest. Some, like the golden plover, which winters in Patagonia, have traveled almost the length of two continents.

A few ducks float on the pools, but there are not nearly so many as in the prairie Provinces farther south. Geese and swans, however, find in these boreal solitudes their main fortress, hundreds of thousands of square miles of lonely land in which to raise their families, safe except for a brief period in summer when they molt their flight feathers. Then the Eskimos drive them like sheep into their traps. The goose which has probably suffered most from these Eskimo drives is the emperor goose (lower left), which lives close to the sea on the west coast of Alaska. It migrates just a short distance to its wintering ground on the southwest coast of Alaska where the Aleutian chain starts. Once in a while a straggler turns up in California. It is therefore the least-known American goose.

Snowy owls, rough-legged hawks, jaegers, and other winged predators feast on the lemming hordes, but the magnificent gyrfalcon would rather have faster fare—seabirds, shorebirds, and hares. Gyrfalcons seem to be common nowhere in the Arctic except, perhaps, on some of the islands near large

Gyrfalcon

Emperor Goose

182

seabird colonies. In the days of medieval falconry the "gyr" could be flown only by a king or an emperor. The prize of all was the white gyrfalcon shown here. Most white gyrfalcons come from Greenland, which was known in the eleventh century, not by the name Leif Erickson gave it, but as the "Land of the White Falcon."

To the Eskimo the snow bunting is the real harbinger of spring, returning in April to the villages to pick up tidbits while the snow still lies deep. Many snow buntings winter on the prairies and farms of the northern states or in the dunes along the coast.

Redpolls, the little pink-breasted finches of the Arctic, also visit the states, but their invasions are more irregular. They reach us some winters, swarming by hundreds into New England weed-patches and into the fields near the Great Lakes. Several seasons may then pass before another visitation.

The raven, hardier than other birds, remains in its bleak domain, somehow managing to find food all through the lean, bitter months. Riding the updrafts and cruising along the ridges, it is startlingly black in a land where so many other creatures wear white in winter. Eskimos seem to have some taboo against killing the raven.

The ptarmigans, the Arctic grouse that turn white in winter and don snowshoes, come down from the rocky foothills when the snow drifts deep and seek shelter among the dwarf willows. There are two kinds in the Arctic, the rock ptarmigan, which in summer lives on the highest, most rugged ridges, and the willow ptarmigan which finds the moors lower down more to its liking.

Eastern Snow Bunting

Common Redpoll

Northern Raven

Willow Ptarmigan

INDEX

This index is keyed to the pages on which the illustrations appear. The text is usually on the same page.

Only English names are indexed by page numbers. The scientific name is indented under each English name but is not cross-indexed.

The letters in brackets are the initials of the artist who executed the illustration. For a key list of these artists refer to the front of the book.

Grouse, Sharp-tailed,
[LBH] 138
  Pediœcetes phasianellus
Grouse, Sooty, [WW] 171
  Dendragapus fuliginosus
Grouse, Spruce, [WW] 73
  Canachites canadensis
Grunt, Yellow, [WW] 134
  Hæmulon sciurus
Gull, Franklin's, [RTP] 141
  Larus pipixcan
Gull, Laughing, [HC] 110
  Larus atricilla
Gyrfalcon, White, [RTP] 182
  Falco rusticolus

Halibut, [FLJ] 117
  Hippoglossus hippoglossus
Hardhead, [FLJ] 117
  Micropogen undulatus
Harebell, [LR] 158
  Campanula rotundifolia
Hawk, Duck, [WW] 110
  Falco peregrinus
Hawk, Marsh, [WW] 104
  Circus cyaneus
Hawk, Red-tailed, [FLJ] 59
  Buteo jamaicensis
Hawkweed, Orange, [WW] 52
  Hieracium aurantiacum
Hemlock, [LR] 67
  Tsuga canadensis
Hen, Heath, [WW] 13
  Tympanuchus cupido
Hen, Sage, [LBH] 171
  Centrocercus urophasianus
Hepatica, Round-lobed, [LR] 47
  Hepatica americana
Heron, Black-crowned Night,
[FLJ] 105
  Nycticorax nycticorax
Heron, Little Blue, [WW] 129
  Florida cærulea
Hickory, White, [FLJ] 42
  Carya glabra
Holly, American, [LR] 121
  Ilex opaca
Honeysuckle, Trumpet, [LR] 26
  Lonicera sempervirens
Hummingbird, Blue-throated,
[WW] 151
  Lampornis clemenciæ
Hummingbird, Ruby-throated,
[WW] 35
  Archilochus colubris
Hyacinth, Water, [MM] 99
  Eichornia crassipes

Ibis, White, [WW] 130
  Guara alba
Indian Pipe, [WW] 68
  Monotropa uniflora
Iris, Blue Flag, [WW] 97
  Iris versicolor
Ironweed, [WW] 29
  Vernonia altissima

Jacana, [WW] 130
  Jacana spinosa
Jack-in-the-Pulpit, [LR] 49
  Arisæma atrorubens
Jaguar, [WW] 133
  Felis hernandesii
Jay, Steller's, [RTP] 167
  Cyanocitta stelleri

Joe-pye Weed, [WW] 29
  Eupatorium dubium
Juniper, Utah, [WW] 155
  Juniperus utahensis

Killdeer, [LBH] 36
  Charadrius vociferus
Kingfisher, Belted, [WW] 83
  Megaceryle alcyon
Kinglet, Ruby-crowned,
[WW] 72
  Regulus calendula
Kite, Mississippi, [WW] 128
  Ictinia misissippiensis

Lady's Slipper, Pink, [LR] 49
  Cypripedium acaule
Lady's Slipper, Showy,
[WW] 95
  Cypripedium reginæ
Lady's-slipper, Yellow,
[WW] 49
  Cypripedium pubescens
Lark, Horned, [WW] 37
  Eremophila alpestris
Laurel, Mountain, [WW] 50
  Kalmia latifolia
Lemming, Collared, [FLJ] 181
  Dicrostonyx rubricatus
Lily, Canada, [LR] 27
  Lilium canadense
Lily, Swamp, [WW] 124
  Crinum americanum
Linden, American, [FLJ] 45
  Tilia americana
Lizard, Collared, [WW] 148
  Chrotaphytus collaris
Lobster, [WW] 114
  Homarus americanus
Locust, Honey, [FLJ] 23
  Gleditsia triacanthos
Loon, Common, [WW] 82
  Gavia immer
Lotus, American, [LR] 98
  Nelumbo lutea
Lupine, [LR] 27
  Lupinus perennis

Mackerel, [FLJ] 117
  Scomber scombrus
Magnolia, [FLJ] 121
  Magnolia sp.
Magpie, [WW] 166
  Pica pica
Mallard, [RTP] 103
  Anas platyrhynchos
Mallow, Swamp Rose, [LR] 97
  Hibiscus palustris
Mammoth, [WW] 12
  Elephas primigenius
Manta, Pacific, [FLJ] 174
  Manta birostris
Mantis, Praying, [WW] 28
  Mantis religiosa
Maple, Silver, [FLJ] 77
  Acer saccharinum
Maple, Sugar, [LR] 23
  Acer saccharum
Marigold, Marsh, [FB] 97
  Caltha palustris
Mariposa, Desert, [LR] 147
  Calochortus kennedyi
Marlin, Blue, [WW] 134
  Makaira nigricans
Marmot, Hoary, [WW] 161
  Marmota caligata

Marten, Pine, [WW] 71
  Martes americana
Martin, Purple, [FLJ] 32
  Progne subis
Meadowlark, [WW] 37
  Sturnella magna
Merganser, American,
[WW] 81
  Mergus merganser
Merganser, Hooded, [WW] 81
  Lophodytes cucullatus
Merrybells, Big, [WW] 48
  Uvularia grandiflora
Milkweed, Common, [MM] 25
  Asclepias syriaca
Mink, [FE] 79
  Mustela vison
Mockingbird, [RTP] 126
  Mimus polyglottos
Moose, [WW] 70
  Alces americana
Moth, Cecropia, [WW] 53
  Samia cecropia
Moth, Luna, [ADC] 53
  Tropæa luna
Moth, Polyphemus, [WW] 53
  Telea polyphemus
Moth, Regal, [WW] 53
  Citheronia regalis
Mouse, White-footed,
[FLJ] 31
  Peromyscus leucopus
Mulberry, Red, [FLJ] 23
  Morus rubra
Muskellunge, [FE] 91
  Esox masquinongy
Musk Ox, [WW] 181
  Ovibos moschatus
Muskrat, [WW] 79
  Ondatra zibethica

Newt, Red, [FLJ] 54
  Triturus viridescens
Nighthawk, [WW] 139
  Chordeiles minor
Nuthatch, Red-breasted,
[WW] 73
  Sitta canadensis

Oak, Live, [FLJ] 120
  Quercus myrtifolia
Oak, Red, [LR] 42
  Quercus rubra
Ocelot, [WW] 133
  Felis pardalis
Ocotillo, [LR] 146
  Fouquiera splendens
Old-Squaw, [WW] 113
  Clangula hyemalis
Opossum, [FE] 57
  Didelphis virginiana
Orange, Osage, [FLJ] 23
  Maclura pomifera
Orchis, Showy, [LR] 49
  Orchis spectabile
Oriole, Baltimore, [RTP] 33
  Icterus galbula
Oriole, Bullock's, [WW] 165
  Icterus bullocki
Oriole, Scott's, [RTP] 150
  Icterus parisorum
Osprey, [WW] 83
  Pandion haliaëtus
Otter, [FLJ] 78
  Lutra canadensis

189

THE PETERSON
FIELD GUIDE SERIES

A FIELD GUIDE TO THE BIRDS by Roger Tory Peterson
Awarded the Brewster Medal.
The standard book for the field identification of the birds of eastern and central North America. The indispensable "bible" of both beginners and experts. 1000 illustrations, 500 in full color.

A FIELD GUIDE TO WESTERN BIRDS by Roger Tory Peterson
The standard western guide using Peterson's unique Field Guide System. 740 illustrations, many in color.

A FIELD GUIDE TO THE SHELLS
of our Atlantic and Gulf Coasts by Percy A. Morris
The beach comber's companion. Beautifully illustrated with over 1000 natural photographs, many in full color.

A FIELD GUIDE TO THE BUTTERFLIES by Alexander B. Klots
A key book in the series. A guide to field natural history as illustrated by the butterflies. Every species north of the Mexican boundary and east of the 100th meridian. 247 species illustrated in full color, and 232 photographs.

A FIELD GUIDE TO THE MAMMALS
by William H. Burt and Richard Grossenheider
All North American mammals north of the Mexican boundary, many illustrated in full color for the first time. Lavishly illustrated with color portraits and range maps.

IN PREPARATION

A FIELD GUIDE TO THE TREES AND SHRUBS by George A. Petrides
A FIELD GUIDE TO THE ROCKS AND MINERALS by Frederick H. Pough

A FIELD GUIDE TO WILDFLOWERS
of the Northeastern and Central States
by Margaret McKenny and Roger Tory Peterson
A FIELD GUIDE TO AMPHIBIANS AND REPTILES
by Roger Conant

THE FIELD GUIDE SERIES

When the original *Field Guide to the Birds* appeared in 1934 it met with instant success. Reviewers hailed it as revolutionary, confirming my most earnest hopes for the book — that it would make quicker, more accurate identification possible in the field. The basic formula, in a nutshell, was *field marks; patterns;* and *distinctions between similar species.*

It was inevitable that nature students everywhere should urge me and my publisher, Houghton Mifflin Company, to extend this system to other branches of nature and to prepare other guides. Thus this series, of which I have accepted editorial responsibility, was launched.

The modern approach to the out-of-doors is the all-embracing one of ecology—the wildlife community. But to understand the community one must first know who the inhabitants are. The Field Guides act as a Who's Who of the wildwood, a short-cut to recognition. The series, a number of titles of which are now being prepared by outstanding specialists, will take its place as the core of every working nature library.

ROGER TORY PETERSON